DAY HIKES AROUND

Sedona
ARIZONA

100 GREAT HIKES

Robert Stone
2nd EDITION

Day Hike Books, Inc.
RED LODGE, MONTANA

Published by Day Hike Books, Inc.
P.O. Box 865 · Red Lodge, Montana 59068
www.dayhikebooks.com

Distributed by National Book Network
800-462-6420 (direct order) · 800-820-2329 (fax order)

Photographs by Robert Stone
Design and Illustrations by Paula Doherty

The author has made every attempt to provide accurate information in this book. However, trail routes and features may change—please use common sense and forethought, and be mindful of your own capabilities. Let this book guide you, but be aware that each hiker assumes responsibility for their own safety. The author and publisher do not assume any responsibility for loss, damage, or injury caused through the use of this book.

Library of Congress Control Number: 2005923476

10 9 8 7 6 5 4 3

Cover photo: The Crimson Cliffs, Hikes 77—79.

Back cover photo: The spires of Twin Buttes at Chicken Point, Hikes 81—84.

Table of Contents

THE HIKES

Oak Creek Canyon

Schnebly Hill Road

Sedona Area
Uptown Sedona • West Sedona • Between the "Y"

Canyon Country: The Dry Creek Area

Highway 179 Access:
Sedona "Y" to the Village of Oak Creek
Marg's Draw • Cathedral Rock • Bell Rock • Courthouse Butte

Hiking Sedona
and the Red Rock Country

T here is an old saying, "God created the Grand Canyon, but he lives in Sedona." The Sedona region is visually stunning. There are extraordinary red rock formations, natural arches, bridges, majestic pinnacles, hanging cliffs, cool gorges, dozens of sculpted canyons, sink holes, mesas with panoramic views, caves with prehistoric pictographs, and 13th century Sinagua Indian ruins, plus year-round creeks and swimming holes. The varied terrain is located in a small geographic area of 25 square miles. This is where the desert meets the forest, between the southern edge of the vast Colorado Plateau, rich with the colorful geography of the Grand Canyon, and the northern edge of the Verde Valley farmland.

Sedona is commonly referred to as the "Grand Canyon you can live in." The town was established in 1902. It sits at an elevation of 4,500 feet above sea level in central Arizona, 120 miles north of Phoenix and 30 miles south of Flagstaff. Sedona is an upscale resort destination, a thriving art colony, and a New Age "energy vortex center" with numerous spiritual sites. It ranks second, only to the Grand Canyon, as the most visited and scenic area in Arizona.

The surrounding landscape, with erosion-sculpted red rocks rising as high as 2,000 feet above the valley floor, is frequently used by Hollywood as a backdrop depicting the Old West. Dozens of western films have brought noted actors such as John Wayne, Jimmy Stewart, Henry Fonda, Burt Lancaster, and Elvis Presley to the area.

Sedona offers an abundance of outdoor activities. You may explore Sedona by jeep, hot air balloon, helicopter, airplane, and, of course, hiking. The unbelievable topography, plus the unique selection and diversity of trails, make hiking one of Sedona's most popular activities. Other activities such as golf, horseback riding, fishing, swimming in natural pools and water slides, bicycling, and camping are all easily accessible. The mild climate makes it possible to enjoy these outdoor activities all year around.

Sedona is surrounded by the Coconino National Forest, which covers more than two million acres. Within the national forest are two protected wilderness areas—the 43,950-acre Red Rock–

Secret Mountain Wilderness and Munds Mountain Wilderness, encompassing another 18,150 acres.

Day Hikes Around Sedona is a comprehensive guide to 100 day hikes within 12 miles of Sedona. Each hike includes a detailed map, accurate driving and hiking directions, and a quick overview of distance/time/elevation. Hikes range from one hour to all day. Relevant maps, including U.S.G.S. topographic maps, are listed with each hike if you wish to explore more of the area. A quick glance at the hikes' summaries will allow you to choose a hike that is appropriate to your ability and desire.

The major access roads around Sedona and to all the hikes are U.S. Highway 89A and Arizona State Highway 179. These two highways intersect in the heart of Sedona. This junction is referred to as the "Y." The driving distances to each hike are measured from the Sedona Y.

RED ROCK PASSES are required parking passes for all the trails in the national forest around Sedona. The fees are used for trail upgrades, restoration, maintainance, protection, and improved signage.

Oak Creek Canyon to Schnebly Hill Road
HIKES 1—23

To the north along Highway 89A is Oak Creek Canyon. This 16-mile canyon has 1,200-foot steep sandstone walls. The multicolored cliffs are naturally landscaped with lush riparian forests, making the area especially beautiful in the fall with its brilliant autumnal foliage. Dozens of springs feed Oak Creek, which tumbles year-round down the canyon and through the town of Sedona, forming cascades, waterfalls, and swimming holes. (The popular Slide Rock State Park and its natural slick rock water slide is found in the canyon.) Rand McNally named Oak Creek Canyon one of the most beautiful drives in America.

Schnebly Hill Road lies at southern end of Oak Creek Canyon straight east of the Sedona Y. The road runs along an old cattle route to the top of Schnebly Hill. The route winds through a canyon along the red sandstone cliffs of Mitten Ridge and the "cow pie" mounds.

Sedona Area
HIKES 24—44

Sedona is located in a wide valley surrounded by plateaus that are edged with stunning rock formations. A network of trails adjacent to town can be accessed directly from the city streets or nearby. Trails from the valley lead up the plateaus for unobstructed vistas of the entire Sedona area. Highlights include Devil's Kitchen, Seven Sacred Pools, Soldier Pass Arches, Coffeepot Rock, and vortex sites atop Airport Mesa.

Red Rock State Park
HIKES 45—49

The state park is a 286-acre nature preserve and education center surrounded by red sandstone mesas. Six miles of well-maintained hiking trails lead through meadows, canyons, across ridges, and up to overlooks with stunning vistas.

Canyon Country
HIKES 50—76

To the west of Sedona along Highway 89A is Canyon Country. Much of the area lies within the Red Rock Secret Mountain Wilderness. There are dozens of colorful, hidden canyons with trails to mesas, arches, spires, and towering red rock formations. In the 12th and 13th Centuries, the Sinagua Indians built their homes among these canyons in natural caves using rock and mud mortar. Highlights include Vultee Arch, Devil's Bridge, the Cockscomb, Boynton Canyon, secluded backcountry hikes, and the Palatki and Honanki archeological sites.

Highway 179: Sedona to the Village of Oak Creek
HIKES 77—100

To the south along Highway 179 is dry, open terrain with world class red rock formations. To the east lies the Munds Mountain Wilderness. The eroded sedimentary formations, including Cathedral Rock, Bell Rock, Courthouse Butte, Snoopy Rock, Camel Head, and the Crimson Cliffs (cover photo), are more than 350-million-years old. Hiking trails run throughout the beautiful red rock basin, adjacent to sandstone formations that rise hundreds of feet above the valley floor.

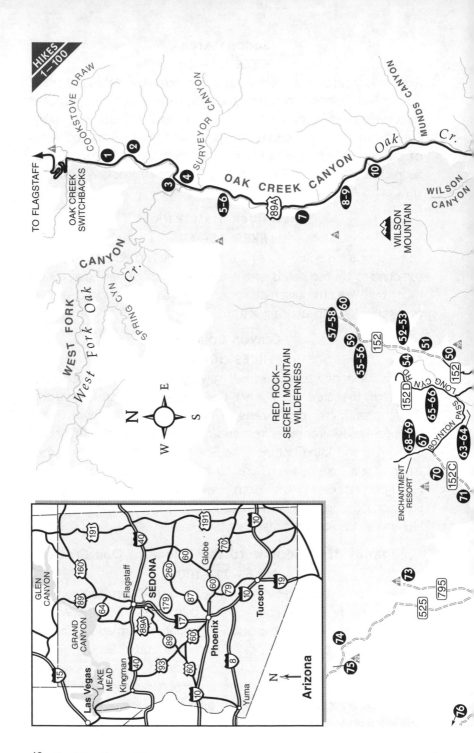

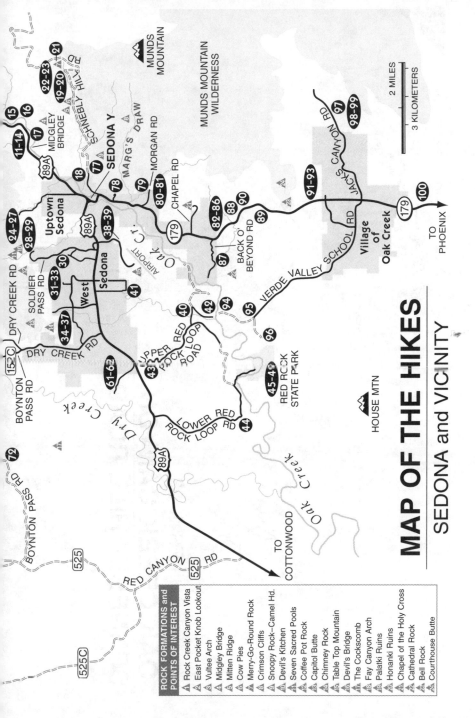

MAP OF THE HIKES
SEDONA and VICINITY

2 MILES
3 KILOMETERS

MUNDS MOUNTAIN
MUNDS MOUNTAIN WILDERNESS

MIDGLEY BRIDGE
SCHNEBLY HILL RD
SEDONA Y
MARG'S DRAW
MORGAN RD
CHAPEL RD
Uptown Sedona
89A
BACK O' BEYOND RD
VERDE VALLEY SCHOOL RD
JACKS CANYON RD
Village of Oak Creek
179
TO PHOENIX

AIRPORT
West Sedona
Oak Creek
SOLDIER PASS RD
DRY CREEK RD
152C
DRY CREEK RD
BOYNTON PASS RD
BOYNTON PASS RD
525
RED CANYON RD
525C
89A
TO COTTONWOOD
Oak Creek
Dry Creek
UPPER RED ROCK LOOP ROAD
LOWER RED ROCK LOOP RD
RED ROCK STATE PARK
HOUSE MTN

<table>
<tr><td colspan="2">ROCK FORMATIONS and POINTS OF INTEREST</td></tr>
<tr><td>△</td><td>Rock Creek Canyon Vista</td></tr>
<tr><td>△</td><td>East Pocket Knob Lookout</td></tr>
<tr><td>△</td><td>Vultee Arch</td></tr>
<tr><td>△</td><td>Midgley Bridge</td></tr>
<tr><td>△</td><td>Mitten Ridge</td></tr>
<tr><td>△</td><td>Cow Pies</td></tr>
<tr><td>△</td><td>Merry-Go-Round Rock</td></tr>
<tr><td>△</td><td>Crimson Cliffs</td></tr>
<tr><td>△</td><td>Snoopy Rock–Camel Hd.</td></tr>
<tr><td>△</td><td>Devil's Kitchen</td></tr>
<tr><td>△</td><td>Seven Sacred Pools</td></tr>
<tr><td>△</td><td>Coffee Pot Rock</td></tr>
<tr><td>△</td><td>Capitol Butte</td></tr>
<tr><td>△</td><td>Chimney Rock</td></tr>
<tr><td>△</td><td>Table Top Mountain</td></tr>
<tr><td>△</td><td>The Cockscomb</td></tr>
<tr><td>△</td><td>Devil's Bridge</td></tr>
<tr><td>△</td><td>Fay Canyon Arch</td></tr>
<tr><td>△</td><td>Palatki Ruins</td></tr>
<tr><td>△</td><td>Honanki Ruins</td></tr>
<tr><td>△</td><td>Chapel of the Holy Cross</td></tr>
<tr><td>△</td><td>Cathedral Rock</td></tr>
<tr><td>△</td><td>Bell Rock</td></tr>
<tr><td>△</td><td>Courthouse Butte</td></tr>
</table>

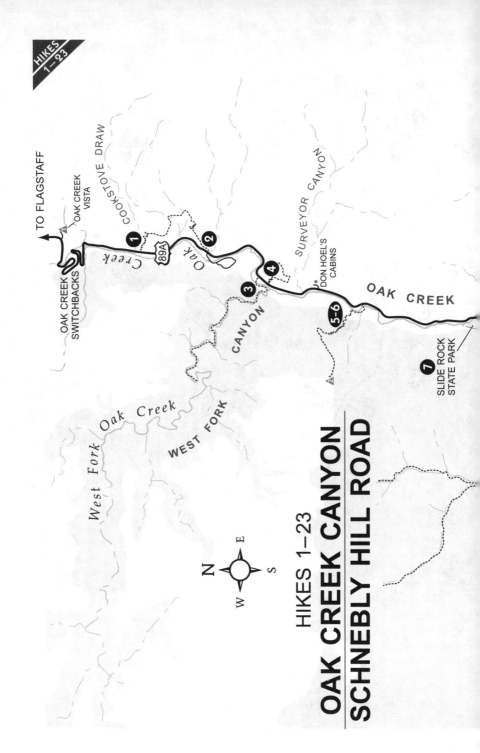

TO FLAGSTAFF

OAK CREEK VISTA

COOKSTOVE DRAW

SURVEYOR CANYON

OAK CREEK SWITCHBACKS

Oak Creek

89A

Oak

CANYON

DON HOEL'S CABINS

OAK CREEK

1

2

3

4

5–6

7

SLIDE ROCK STATE PARK

West Fork Oak Creek

West Fork

WEST FORK

N
E
S
W

HIKES 1–23
OAK CREEK CANYON
SCHNEBLY HILL ROAD

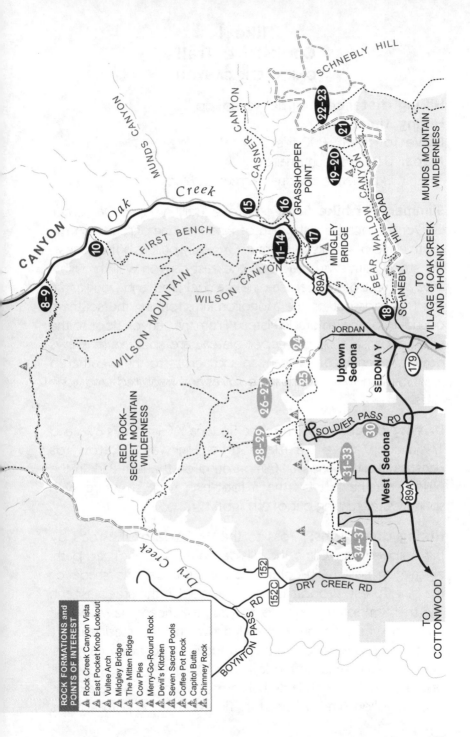

ROCK FORMATIONS and
POINTS OF INTEREST
🔺 Rock Creek Canyon Vista
🔺 East Pocket Knob Lookout
🔺 Vultee Arch
🔺 Midgley Bridge
🔺 The Mitten Ridge
🔺 Cow Pies
🔺 Devil's Kitchen
🔺 Seven Sacred Pools
🔺 Coffee Pot Rock
🔺 Capitol Butte
🔺 Chimney Rock

Hike 1
Cookstove Trail
OAK CREEK CANYON

Hiking distance: 1.6 miles round trip
Hiking time: 1 hour
Elevation gain: 800 feet
Maps: U.S.G.S. Mountainaire
Experience Sedona Recreation Map

Summary of hike: The Cookstove Trail, in upper Oak Creek Canyon, is located just north of Pine Flat Campground on the south edge of Cookstove Draw. Originally built as a fire access, the steep path switchbacks up the east canyon wall through a shady forest of Ponderosa pine, gambel pine, and Douglas fir. The trail tops out on the Mogollon Rim, forming the southern boundary of the Colorado Plateau. From the canyon floor to the open expanse atop the upper plateau are spectacular views down the length of the canyon and across to the weathered west canyon wall with chiseled spires and fractured sandstone cliffs.

Driving directions: From the Sedona Y (Highways 89A and 179 junction), drive 12.8 miles north on Highway 89A (towards Flagstaff) to the Pine Flat Campground on the left. Park in the pullout on the left by the 5-foot-high rock structure with spring water running out of a spigot.

Hiking directions: Cross to the east side of the road by the trailhead sign. Climb the hillside on the well-defined path, zigzagging past multi-colored boulders under the shade of the pine forest. Wood and rock steps aid in the steep ascent. The trail temporarily levels out, with magnificent views of the serrated west canyon wall and down the forested canyon. Continue up the narrow ridge, straddling two deep canyons. Cookstove Draw is on the left (north). At 0.8 miles, near the plateau, wind through large boulders, emerging on the expansive Mogollon Rim in a forest of fir and pines. A path follows the rim to an endless series of overlooks. The unmaintained path, marked with cairns, leads 1.25 miles south and connects with the Harding Springs Trail (Hike 2) for a 4-mile loop. Before you explore the vast expanse, make a mental note of where the Cookstove Trail meets the rim for your return.

TO
FLAGSTAFF

Cookstove Draw

RITTER
BUTTE
6,988'

COOKSTOVE TRAIL

MOGOLLON RIM

P

PINE FLAT
CAMPGROUND

Oak Creek

N
E
W
S

OAK CREEK CANYON

2 TRAIL

HARDING SPRINGS

RED ROCK–
SECRET MOUNTAIN
WILDERNESS

89A

CAVE SPRING
CAMPGROUND

TO
SEDONA

COOKSTOVE TRAIL
OAK CREEK CANYON

Hike 2
Harding Springs Trail
OAK CREEK CANYON

Hiking distance: 1.6 miles round trip
Hiking time: 1 hour
Elevation gain: 900 feet
Maps: U.S.G.S. Mountainaire and Munds Park
Experience Sedona Recreation Map

Summary of hike: The Harding Springs Trail in Oak Creek Canyon climbs from the canyon floor by Cave Spring Campground to the east rim. The canyon-to-rim trail was named for homesteader Colonel O.P. Harding, who lived where the Cave Spring Campground is today. The trail was built in the 1880s as a direct access to Flagstaff and as a summer pasturing route for cattle. The path climbs under a canopy of ponderosa pine and Douglas fir to the Mogollon Rim on the southern edge of the Colorado Plateau. From the upper plateau are great views across the canyon. To the north, an unmaintained trail connects with the Cookstove Trail (Hike 1) for a 4-mile loop.

Driving directions: From the Sedona Y (Highways 89A and 179 junction), drive 11.7 miles north on Highway 89A (towards Flagstaff) to the Cave Spring Campground on the left. Park in the small pullouts on the left side of the road.

Hiking directions: The posted trailhead is directly across the road from the paved campground entrance. Take the trail on the east side of the highway, and head into the pine forest. Traverse the hillside to the northeast, steadily gaining elevation under the shade of the forest to the edge of a side canyon. Switchback to the right and continue climbing the mountain along a series of nine switchbacks. Emerge on a large, grassy flat by a wooden post in an open forest of pines and fir. Rocks line the path leading into a meadow. A south-facing overlook sits at the edge of the rim, perched high above the canyon floor. This is the turn-around spot.

To hike farther, a faint path curves left from the post at the top of the Harding Springs Trail. Widely spaced cairns mark the northbound path, which connects with the Cookstove Trail (Hike 1) in 1.25 miles.

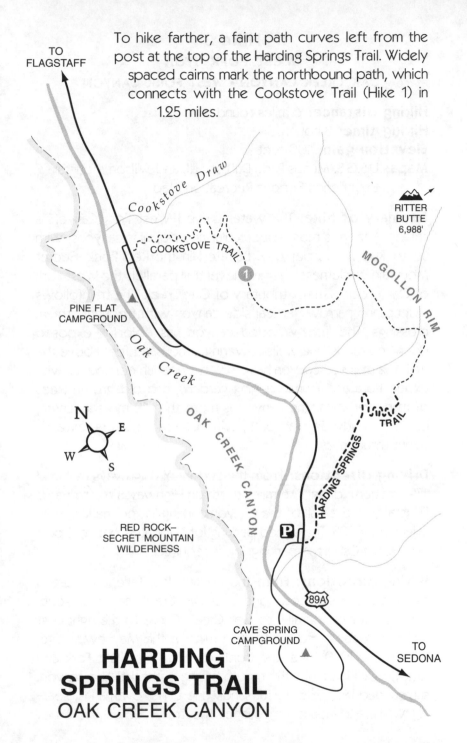

TO
FLAGSTAFF

Cookstove Draw

RITTER
BUTTE
6,988'

COOKSTOVE TRAIL ①

MOGOLLON RIM

PINE FLAT
CAMPGROUND

Oak Creek

OAK CREEK CANYON

HARDING SPRINGS TRAIL

N
E
W
S

RED ROCK–
SECRET MOUNTAIN
WILDERNESS

P

89A

CAVE SPRING
CAMPGROUND

TO
SEDONA

HARDING SPRINGS TRAIL
OAK CREEK CANYON

Hike 3
West Fork Trail
OAK CREEK CANYON · WEST FORK CANYON

Hiking distance: 6 miles round trip
Hiking time: 3 hours
Elevation gain: 100 feet
Maps: U.S.G.S. Munds Park, Dutton Hill, and Wilson Mountain
  Experience Sedona Recreation Map

Summary of hike: The water-carved West Fork Canyon is among Arizona's most spectacular and popular canyons, with up to 300 hikers per day. Located in the Red Rock–Secret Mountain Wilderness, this near level trail parallels the West Fork of Oak Creek, a major tributary of Oak Creek. The trail follows a deep and narrow vertical side canyon with frequent stream crossings. The lush, wooded canyon has colorful, exposed Coconino sandstone walls towering a thousand feet above the trail. The majestic canyon has a diverse riparian community with exotic flora and fauna, hanging gardens, and old-grown trees of many varieties. The canyon is more than 12 miles in length, but the clearly defined path, with half-mile markers, extends about three miles.

Driving directions: From the Sedona Y (Highways 89A and 179 junction), drive 10.6 miles north on Highway 89A (towards Flagstaff) to the Call of the Canyon parking lot on the left, near mile marker 385. The signed parking lot is located one mile past Don Hoel's Cabins. A parking fee is required.

Hiking directions: From the parking lot, take the posted trail west. Cross a footbridge over Oak Creek, and head south a short distance, parallel to Oak Creek. Curve to the right past a red rock cabin and the burned ruins of the Mayhew Lodge, built in the 1930s near the confluence of the West Fork and Oak Creek. Head into the mouth of the cathedral-like canyon, surrounded by the colorful sandstone cliffs, overhangs, soaring walls, and abundant foliage. The trail follows the creek between the narrow erosion-carved cliffs along terra-cotta slick rock, criss-crossing over the shallow creek on stepping stones. At 2 miles, pass under a wave-shaped overhang, known as Wave Cave. At about 3 miles, the easy-to-follow trail ends at a pool. This is a good turn-around spot.

To hike farther, the route entails boulder hopping, wading across wall-to-wall pools, and bushwhacking through overgrown vegetation.

West Fork

of Oak Creek

WEST FORK CANYON

N
W   E
S

TO
FLAGSTAFF

RED ROCK–
SECRET MOUNTAIN
WILDERNESS

CAVE SPRING
CAMPGROUND

P

Oak Creek

OAK CREEK CANYON

89A

THOMAS
△ POINT

4

WEST FORK
TRAIL

TO
SEDONA

DON HOEL'S
CABINS

Hike 4
Thomas Point Trail
OAK CREEK CANYON

Hiking distance: 2.4 miles round trip
Hiking time: 1.5 hours
Elevation gain: 900 feet
Maps: U.S.G.S. Munds Park
Beartooth Publishing—Sedona, AZ

Summary of hike: The Thomas Point Trail is a steep ascent up Oak Creek Canyon's vertical east wall. C.S. "Bear" Howard, the first Anglo settler in upper Oak Creek Canyon, pioneered the trail back in the 1870s. It was named after John "Dad" Thomas, who purchased the ranch in 1888, and was originally used to bring supplies and lumber back from Flagstaff. The path climbs switchbacks from the canyon floor through an evergreen forest up to the towering eastern ramparts and a lookout point on the Mogollon Rim. From the lookout are views north of the majestic 13,000-foot San Francisco Peaks, the red rock walls across the Oak Creek Canyon, the cliffs at the mouth of the West Fork Canyon, East Pocket, and Wilson Mountain.

Driving directions: From the Sedona Y (Highways 89A and 179 junction), drive 10.6 miles north on Highway 89A (towards Flagstaff) to the Call of the Canyon parking lot on the left, near mile marker 385. The parking lot is located one mile past Don Hoel's Cabins. A parking fee is required.

Hiking directions: From the parking lot, walk down canyon along Highway 89A for less than a quarter mile to the posted Thomas Point Trailhead on the left (east). The sign is up the trail about 15 feet off the road. The trail immediately begins its steep ascent. Climb a continuous series of vertical switchbacks through the forest. At a half mile, the path winds to the sunny south face with chaparral and juniper. From here, the steep grade eases up to the plateau atop the Mogollon Rim on the east edge of the canyon. Cairns mark the path north to the Thomas Point lookout, perched on a west-pointing rock outcrop.

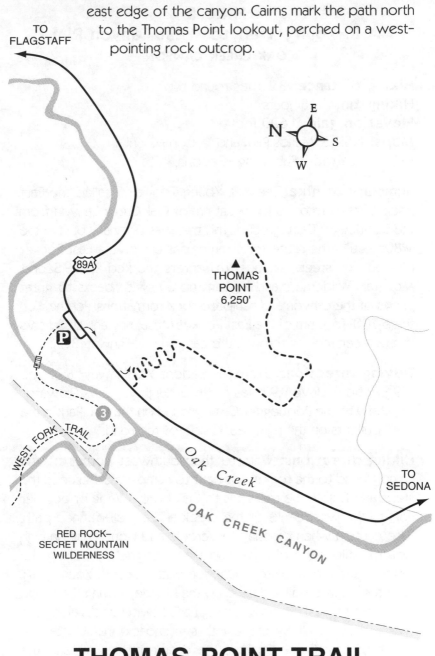

THOMAS POINT TRAIL
OAK CREEK CANYON

Hike 5
A.B. Young Trail to West Canyon Rim
OAK CREEK CANYON

Hiking distance: 3.2 miles round trip
Hiking time: 1.5 hours
Elevation gain: 1,600 feet
Maps: U.S.G.S. Munds Park and Wilson Mountain
      Beartooth Publishing—Sedona, AZ

Summary of hike: The A.B. Young Trail (also called the East Pocket Trail) climbs to the west rim of Oak Creek Canyon from the Bootlegger Campground. The trail was originally built in the 1880s as a cattle route for summer pasture on the East Pocket plateau. The steep, sinuous trail enters the Red Rock—Secret Mountain Wilderness and zigzags up 33 switchbacks to great views of the canyon and sculpted rock formations. Perched on the 6,700-foot rim of the East Pocket Mesa, tiny ant-sized cars can be seen moving through the canyon on Highway 89A.

Driving directions: From the Sedona Y (Highways 89A and 179 junction), drive 8.9 miles north on Highway 89A (towards Flagstaff) to the Bootlegger Campground on the left. Park in the small pullouts on the right (east) side of the road.

Hiking directions: Walk to the southwest corner of the campground to the rock steps next to campsite 5. Descend the steps and follow the trail signs to Oak Creek. Wade or boulder hop to the west banks of the creek and a well-defined path. (Use caution when crossing the creek, and don't cross in high water.) Follow the old road upstream to the right along the base of the mountain to a junction with the A.B. Young Trail. Take the posted trail and head up the hillside, leaving the shade of the pine forest. Steadily zigzag up 33 switchbacks along the west canyon wall. By the eighth switchback are spectacular views of Oak Creek Canyon, the east canyon wall, and the jagged sandstone sculptures above. Continue uphill, passing and climbing above the eroding spires that were in view from below. At 1.6 miles, top the rim into a pine grove strewn with boulders and a log to sit on. Rest and savor the views extending across the forested plateau. This is our turn-around spot.

To hike farther, continue with the next hike to the East Pocket Knob Fire Lookout Tower.

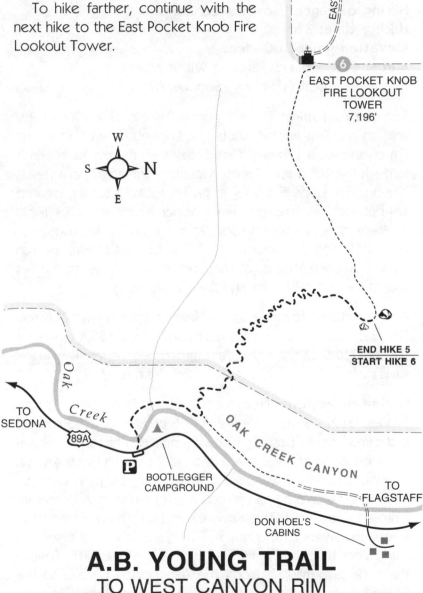

EAST POCKET ROAD

6

EAST POCKET KNOB
FIRE LOOKOUT
TOWER
7,196'

W
S ◇ N
E

END HIKE 5
START HIKE 6

Oak

Creek

TO
SEDONA

89A

OAK CREEK CANYON

P

BOOTLEGGER
CAMPGROUND

DON HOEL'S
CABINS

TO
FLAGSTAFF

A.B. YOUNG TRAIL
TO WEST CANYON RIM

Hike 6
A. B. Young Trail to
East Pocket Knob Fire Lookout Tower
OAK CREEK CANYON

Hiking distance: 5.6 miles round trip
Hiking time: 3 hours
Elevation gain: 2,000 feet
Maps: U.S.G.S. Munds Park and Wilson Mountain
Beartooth Publishing—Sedona, AZ

Summary of hike: The A.B. Young Trail climbs 2,000 vertical feet to the East Pocket Knob Fire Lookout Tower. From the rim on the west edge of Oak Creek Canyon, the path winds through the Red Rock–Secret Mountain Wilderness in a forest of ponderosa pine and Douglas fir. The lookout tower, located just outside the wilderness, is a wooden structure with 3 flights of steps to an enclosed room at the top. The lookout provides 360-degree panoramas of Oak Creek Canyon; the San Francisco Peaks; Mingus, Wilson, and Munds Mountains; the flat top of the Mogollon Rim; and the Verde Valley.

Driving directions: From the Sedona Y (Highways 89A and 179 junction), drive 8.9 miles north on Highway 89A (towards Flagstaff) to the Bootlegger Campground on the left. Park in the small pullouts on the right (east) side of the road.

Hiking directions: From the top of the rim on the west side of Oak Creek Canyon—where Hike 5 ends—curve southwest and climb into the partial shade of a pine and fir forest. Parallel the west edge of the canyon. Meander through the forest on a gentle uphill grade with rock cairns marking the path. Climb to a flat knoll by an old trail sign and a 3-foot-high rock cairn with a rim-edge overlook. The views extend south and west across layers and layers of mountains. Fifty yards ahead is a second cairn. Veer to the right, leaving the edge of the cliffs. Follow the rock cairn markers along the flat-topped plateau to the lookout tower at the end of the unpaved East Pocket Road.

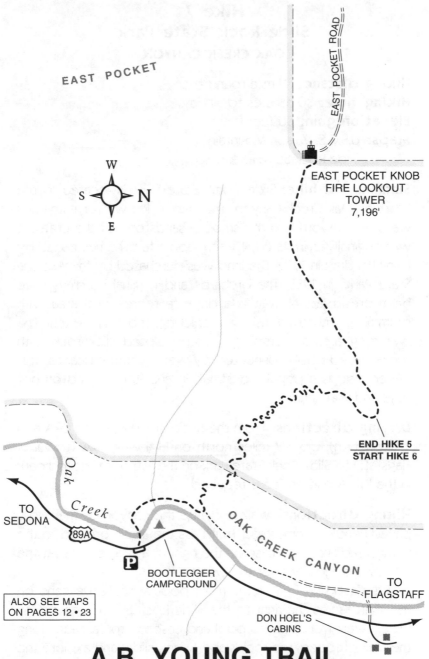

EAST POCKET

W N S E

EAST POCKET ROAD

EAST POCKET KNOB
FIRE LOOKOUT
TOWER
7,196'

END HIKE 5
START HIKE 6

Oak Creek

TO
SEDONA

89A

OAK CREEK CANYON

P

BOOTLEGGER
CAMPGROUND

ALSO SEE MAPS
ON PAGES 12 • 23

TO
FLAGSTAFF

DON HOEL'S
CABINS

A.B. YOUNG TRAIL
TO EAST POCKET KNOB LOOKOUT TOWER

Hike 7
Slide Rock State Park
OAK CREEK CANYON

Hiking distance: 1 mile round trip
Hiking time: 30 minutes to all day
Elevation gain: 50 feet
Maps: U.S.G.S. Wilson Mountain
Slide Rock State Park Map

Summary of hike: Slide Rock State Park is located in the heart of Oak Creek Canyon. The park is known for its natural water slide worn into the smooth sandstone of the creek. It was originally an irrigated, 43-acre apple farm homesteaded by Frank Pendley in 1910. The land was purchased by the Arizona State Parks in 1985. The orchards and original buildings have been preserved. Now it is a day-use recreational area with swimming, sunbathing, fishing, picnicking, and a nature trail. The swimming area has sloping, water-sculpted slick rock with rock-rimmed pools connected by water chute cascades. This water slide is a popular destination and is crowded on hot days and weekends.

Driving directions: From the Sedona Y (Highways 89A and 179 junction), drive 7 miles north on Highway 89A (towards Flagstaff) to Slide Rock State Park on the left. Turn left and park in the lot. A parking fee is required.

Hiking directions: Walk north up the canyon on the wide, paved Pendley Homestead Trail. Pass the apple orchard to the homestead and a staircase on the right at a quarter mile. At the staircase is a junction for the two trails.

THE CREEKSIDE TRAIL is the most popular route. Descend on the staircase to the right to the Slide Rock Swim Area at Oak Creek. Walk from pool to pool and cascade to cascade along the stair-stepped, red rock slabs. Swim, slide, and explore the water park along the bedrock of Oak Creek. This is a play-all-day area.

THE CLIFFTOP NATURE TRAIL leads straight ahead to the north through a meadow with historic apple trees and antique farm machinery. The trail parallels the cliffs overlooking Oak Creek, the canyon, and the pools below. This short loop has well-placed benches for taking in the sights. It returns to the trail junction.

TO
FLAGSTAFF

SLIDE ROCK
SWIM AREA

CLIFFTOP NATURE TRAIL

OVERLOOK

CREEKSIDE TRAIL

CREEKSIDE
STAIRS

Oak Creek

89A

APPLE
ORCHARD

N
W   E
S

ANTIQUE
FARM
MACHINERY

PENDLEY HOMESTEAD TRAIL

CABINS

RANGER
STATION

RED ROCK–
SECRET MOUNTAIN
WILDERNESS

P

ALSO SEE MAPS
ON PAGES 12 • 31

TO
SEDONA

SLIDE ROCK
STATE PARK

Hike 8
Sterling Pass Trail to Sterling Pass
OAK CREEK CANYON

Hiking distance: 3.2 miles round trip
Hiking time: 1.5 hours
Elevation gain: 1,100 feet
Maps: U.S.G.S. Munds Park and Wilson Mountain
Beartooth Publishing—Sedona, AZ

map
next page

Summary of hike: The Sterling Pass Trail, located just north of the Manzanita Campground in Oak Creek Canyon, is said to be an old Indian route. From the west side of the canyon, the trail enters the Red Rock—Secret Mountain Wilderness and heads into a side drainage on the north face of Wilson Mountain. The steep route climbs to 6,000-foot Sterling Pass, a narrow, notched saddle between Wilson Mountain and East Pocket. There are excellent views of the canyon and the rich-red spires. The trail continues down Sterling Canyon (Hike 9), connecting with Vultee Arch (Hike 60) and the Dry Creek Basin at the end of Forest Service Road 152. It can be hiked as a one-way, 4.25-mile shuttle with Hikes 9 and 60.

Driving directions: From the Sedona Y (Highways 89A and 179 junction), drive 6.3 miles north on Highway 89A (towards Flagstaff) to the Manzanita Campground on the right. Park in the small pullouts alongside the road, just past the posted campground entrance.

Hiking directions: The signed trailhead is 100 yards north of the campground on the left (west) side of the road. Immediately climb the hillside on the posted red dirt trail. Enter the canyon beneath the towering red rock formations. Follow the canyon drainage into the Red Rock—Secret Mountain Wilderness under a shaded forest canopy. Leave the canyon floor and climb the north-facing wall, steadily gaining elevation beneath the red rock sculptures. As the trail nears the formidable red cliffs and spires, a series of short switchbacks zigzag up the mountain. Skirt the spires and pass caves on the fine sand and natural rock path to Sterling Pass, a small saddle covered with oaks, maples, and sitting rocks. Views extend east across Oak Creek Canyon and west into Sterling Canyon. This is the turn-around spot.

To hike into Sterling Canyon and view Vultee Arch, continue with the next hike.

Hike 9
Sterling Pass Trail to Vultee Arch
OAK CREEK CANYON

Hiking distance: 5 miles round trip
Hiking time: 3 hours
Elevation gain: 1,900 feet
Maps: U.S.G.S. Munds Park and Wilson Mountain
Beartooth Publishing—Sedona, AZ

map
next page

Summary of hike: The Sterling Pass Trail follows a side canyon of Oak Creek Canyon along the north face of Wilson Mountain. The trail climbs to 6,000-foot Sterling Pass, then descends into Sterling Canyon, a quiet canyon with ponderosa pine, oak, and maple trees. The trail leads to Dry Creek Basin at the end of Forest Service Road 152. A side path leads to a large slab of red rock with an overlook of Vultee Arch, a large 40-foot-high natural bridge stretching 50 feet across the north wall of Sterling Canyon at the base of East Pocket Mesa. This trail can also be combined with Hike 60 to Vultee Arch for a one-way, 4.25-mile shuttle.

Driving directions: From the Sedona Y (Highways 89A and 179 junction), drive 6.3 miles north on Highway 89A (towards Flagstaff) to the Manzanita Campground on the right. Park in the small pullouts alongside the road, just past the posted campground entrance.

For a one-way shuttle hike, leave a second car at the trailhead for Hike 60.

Hiking directions: From Sterling Pass—where Hike 8 ends—descend through ponderosa pines and maples on a soft carpet of needles. Skirt the sculpted red rock formations on the left and head down canyon. A series of switchbacks weave through the forest between the towering cliffs, with an ever-changing view of etched red rock formations, spires, and caves. The stunning scenery makes it hard to keep your eyes on the trail, but the long sweeping switchbacks ensure an easy descent. Continue downhill to the isolated canyon floor with a rich understory of bracken ferns. Follow the drainage beneath the red walls. The Sterling Pass Trail ends at 2.4 miles at a posted junction with the Vultee Arch Trail. The left fork leads 1.6 miles to the parking lot at the end of Dry Creek Road (Hike 60). Take the right fork 70 yards to the Vultee Arch viewpoint on a large red rock knoll. From this clearing, the arch is in full view, directly across the box canyon on the north wall. Return by retracing your steps.

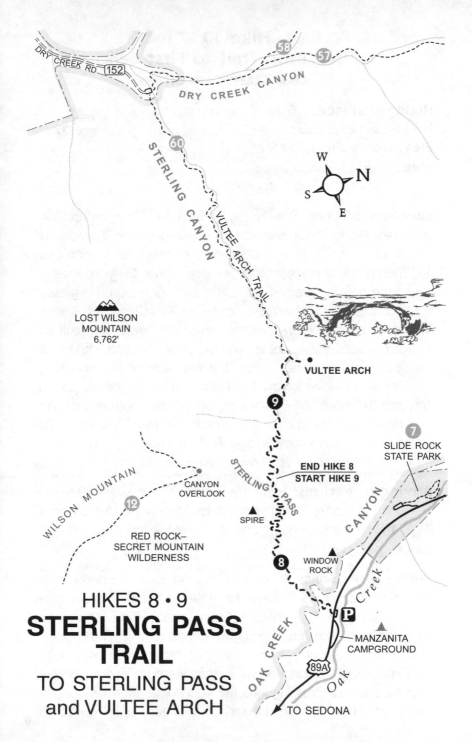

DRY CREEK RD 152

58 57

DRY CREEK CANYON

60

STERLING CANYON

VULTEE ARCH TRAIL

W N
S E

LOST WILSON
MOUNTAIN
6,762'

VULTEE ARCH

9

7
SLIDE ROCK
STATE PARK

WILSON MOUNTAIN

12

CANYON
OVERLOOK

END HIKE 8
START HIKE 9

STERLING PASS

SPIRE

RED ROCK–
SECRET MOUNTAIN
WILDERNESS

CANYON

Creek

8

WINDOW
ROCK

P

MANZANITA
CAMPGROUND

HIKES 8 • 9
STERLING PASS
TRAIL
TO STERLING PASS
and VULTEE ARCH

OAK CREEK

89A

Oak Creek

TO SEDONA

Hike 10
North Wilson Trail to First Bench
OAK CREEK CANYON

Hiking distance: 3.6 miles round trip
Hiking time: 2 hours
Elevation gain: 1,700 feet
Maps: U.S.G.S. Munds Park
      Beartooth Publishing—Sedona, AZ

map
page 37

Summary of hike: The North Wilson Trail begins at the Encinoso Picnic Area and climbs a shady side canyon of Wilson Mountain in the Red Rock—Secret Mountain Wilderness. J.J. Thompson, a homesteader in Oak Creek Canyon, established the trail for grazing his cattle and horses on the grassy mountaintop. The trail zigzags up to the First Bench of Wilson Mountain, a large, sloping plateau formed by the down-fault of a huge block of the mountain. The bench is covered with black basalt lava and stretches across the east side of the mountain, offering great views of the San Francisco Peaks, the Mogollon Rim, and the mouth of Munds Canyon. At the south end of the First Bench, the trail meets the Wilson Mountain Trail (Hike 11) coming up from Midgley Bridge. To hike farther, the trail continues to the top of Wilson Mountain (Hike 12).

Driving directions: From the Sedona Y (Highways 89A and 179 junction), drive 5.3 miles north on Highway 89A (towards Flagstaff) to the Encinoso Picnic Area on the left. Turn left and park in the paved lot.

Hiking directions: Walk to the north end of the parking lot to the trailhead map. Follow the base of the hill a short distance, parallel to Highway 89A. Curve up the hillside and away from the road. Meander through the side canyon in the open forest to a ridge above the Encinoso Picnic Area overlooking Oak Creek Canyon. Follow the ridge south into a ponderosa pine forest, crossing into the Red Rock—Secret Mountain Wilderness. Continue on the steady but easy uphill grade to the sheer wall of Wilson Mountain at one mile. Begin the steep ascent, zigzagging up the north face of Wilson Mountain beneath the towering red sandstone cliffs and numerous sweeping overlooks. As you near the top and the steep grade eases, follow the ridge south onto the First Bench of Wilson Mountain at 1.5 miles. Stroll south across the expansive plateau, with views of Munds Mountain and stream-fed Munds Canyon. Continue to a posted 3-way junction on the south edge of the First Bench. This is our turn-around spot.

To hike farther, the left fork leads downhill on the Wilson Mountain Trail to Midgley Bridge (Hike 11). The right fork leads to upper Wilson Mountain and more expansive views (Hike 12).

Hike 11
Wilson Mountain Trail to First Bench
OAK CREEK CANYON • WILSON CANYON

Hiking distance: 5.6 miles round trip
Hiking time: 3 hours
Elevation gain: 1,600 feet
Maps: U.S.G.S. Munds Park and Wilson Mountain
　　　　Beartooth Publishing—Sedona, AZ

map
page 37

Summary of hike: Wilson Mountain was named for Richard Wilson, mauled and killed by a grizzly bear in 1885. The Wilson Mountain Trail begins by Midgley Bridge at the mouth of Wilson Canyon. The trail climbs the southeast face of the mountain to the First Bench. The bench, stretching along the east side of the mountain, is a down-faulted chunk of land 700 feet below the summit that was originally part of the mountaintop. The trail provides fine views of the Red Rock Country and across Verde Valley. The path intersects with the North Wilson Trail (Hike 10) and continues to the top of Wilson Mountain (Hike 12).

Driving directions: From the Sedona Y (Highways 89A and 179 junction), drive 1.9 miles north on Highway 89A (towards Flagstaff) to the parking lot on the left, just after crossing Midgley Bridge.

Hiking directions: Walk up the canyon 20 yards, passing the trailhead map, to a junction by the picnic tables. The left fork, straight ahead, leads up the floor of Wilson Canyon (Hike 13). Bear right, climbing up the hillside on the east side of the canyon. Follow the red rock path through a mixed forest. The views include Wilson Canyon and the original highway looping around Wilson Canyon before Midgley Bridge was built. Additional views extend across Oak Creek Canyon to the Schnebly Hill formations. The path levels out for a long stretch, passing under two sets of power lines, and heads due north towards the flat-topped First Bench of Wilson Mountain. At 0.75 miles is a posted junction at the Red Rock–Secret Mountain Wilderness boundary. The left fork drops into Wilson Canyon (Hike 14). Stay to the right and continue up the rocky path to the base of the mountain plateau. Curve left (west) to the head of Wilson Canyon, then curve right (northeast) to the foot of Wilson Mountain. At 1.25 miles, begin the steep ascent up switchbacks on the exposed south face. Zigzag up the hillside on the rock-strewn trail that overlooks endless red rock formations, Midgley Bridge, Uptown Sedona, and the Verde Valley floor. Near the top, the grade eases and follows the ridge north onto the First Bench of Wilson Mountain and up to a posted 3-way junction. This is our turn-around spot.

To hike farther, the right fork leads down the north face of Wilson Mountain to the Encinoso Picnic Area in Oak Creek Canyon (Hike 10). The left fork leads to Upper Wilson Mountain and the overlooks (Hike 12).

Hike 12
Wilson Mountain Trail to Canyon and Sedona Overlooks
OAK CREEK CANYON • WILSON CANYON

Hiking distance: 10.6 miles round trip
Hiking time: 5 hours
Elevation gain: 2,400 feet
Maps: U.S.G.S. Munds Park and Wilson Mountain
      Beartooth Publishing—Sedona, AZ

map next page

Summary of hike: Wilson Mountain is the highest mountain in the area, topping out at 7,122 feet. The trail climbs the cliffs from the 6,200-foot First Bench of Wilson Mountain up to the top of the mountain, with incredible overlooks on both the north rim and the south rim. The hike is a continuation of the North Wilson Trail (Hike 10) and the Wilson Mountain Trail (Hike 11). The mountaintop is covered with basaltic lava flows that date back 5 million years. From the summit are bird's-eye views of the entire area from 3,000 feet above the city of Sedona. The 360-degree views include the Verde Valley to the south, the San Francisco Peaks to the north, Oak Creek Canyon and the Mogollon Rim to the east, and the Red Rock Country to the west.

Driving directions: From the Sedona Y (Highways 89A and 179 junction), drive 1.9 miles north on Highway 89A (towards Flagstaff) to the parking lot on the left, just after crossing Midgley Bridge.

Hiking directions: From the posted 3-way junction at the end of Hike 10 or 11, leave the First Bench of Wilson Mountain, and head uphill into a forest of ponderosa pines and gambel oaks. Climb a couple of switchbacks on the gentle uphill grade. The views extend across Oak Creek Canyon, Munds Canyon, and the forested Mogollon Rim. The trail tops out and curves northwest, away from Oak Creek Canyon. Wind through the forest and climb a short distance to a 6,900-foot saddle and a posted junction by a forest service tool shed that stores fire fighting equipment. The left fork leads a half mile to the Sedona Overlook. For now, take the right fork towards the Canyon Overlook 1.4 miles ahead. The level path wends through the forest to the 6,800-foot north edge of Wilson Mountain. The sights include a 2,000-foot deep view into Oak Creek Canyon, Sterling Canyon, and across East Pocket up to the San Francisco Peaks in Flagstaff. A path follows the rim west to views of Lost Wilson Mountain and the Dry Creek Basin. Return to the junction on the saddle by the tool shed. Take the trail that is now on your right, and climb the hill heading south. Skirt around the west side of the 7,045-foot knoll, and drop down through the open pine forest to an overlook on the south edge of Wilson Mountain. Savor the views across the entire Sedona area, from Schnebly Hill to the Village of Oak Creek and from the far reaches of West Sedona to the Verde Valley.

HIKES 10 • 11
FIRST BENCH
NORTH WILSON TRAIL
WILSON MOUNTAIN TRAIL

HIKE 12
WILSON MOUNTAIN TRAIL
TO CANYON and SEDONA OVERLOOKS

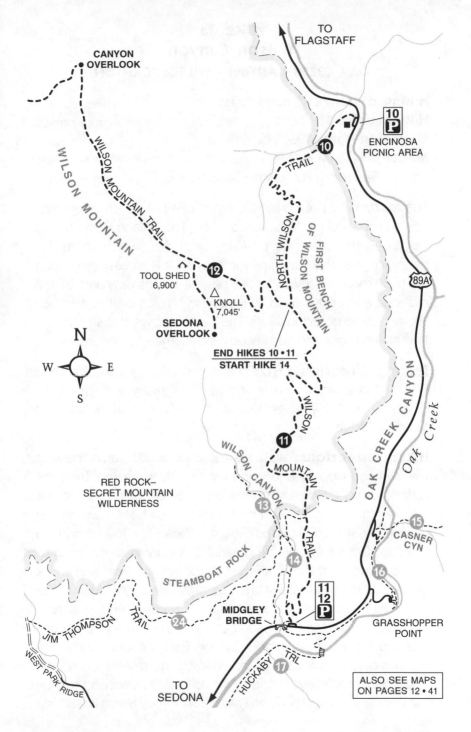

CANYON OVERLOOK

WILSON MOUNTAIN

WILSON MOUNTAIN TRAIL

TO FLAGSTAFF

10 P
ENCINOSA PICNIC AREA

10

TRAIL

NORTH WILSON

FIRST BENCH OF WILSON MOUNTAIN

89A

12

TOOL SHED 6,900'

KNOLL 7,045'

SEDONA OVERLOOK

END HIKES 10 • 11
START HIKE 14

WILSON

11

OAK CREEK CANYON

Oak Creek

N
W   E
S

RED ROCK– SECRET MOUNTAIN WILDERNESS

WILSON CANYON

MOUNTAIN

13

15

CASNER CYN

STEAMBOAT ROCK

TRAIL

14

16

JIM THOMPSON TRAIL

24

MIDGLEY BRIDGE

11 12 P

GRASSHOPPER POINT

WEST PARK RIDGE

TO SEDONA

HUCKABY TRL

17

ALSO SEE MAPS ON PAGES 12 • 41

Hike 13
Wilson Canyon
OAK CREEK CANYON · WILSON CANYON

Hiking distance: 3 miles round trip
Hiking time: 1.5 hours
Elevation gain: 100 feet
Maps: U.S.G.S. Munds Park
Beartooth Publishing—Sedona, AZ

map
next page

Summary of hike: Wilson Canyon is a lush, enchanting canyon surrounded by Wilson Mountain. The Wilson Canyon Trail begins on the east side of Midgley Bridge, which spans the deep gorge at the mouth of the canyon. It is an easy hike along the tree-shaded canyon floor. The trail passes remnants of the old road and bridge used to cross the canyon before Midgley Bridge was erected in 1939. The path follows the streambed through red rock grottos and ends by large rock boulders.

Driving directions: From the Sedona Y (Highways 89A and 179 junction), drive 1.9 miles north on Highway 89A (towards Flagstaff) to the parking lot on the left, just after crossing Midgley Bridge.

Hiking directions: Walk up the canyon 20 yards, passing the trailhead map to a junction by the picnic tables. The right fork heads up the hillside on the east side of the canyon to the First Bench of Wilson Mountain (Hikes 11 and 14). Stay on the wide left path (an old road) straight ahead for 160 yards to a trail fork. Detour left on the original Oak Creek Canyon road to the remnants of the old Wilson Canyon Bridge by a deep rock gorge. (A footpath along the old highway loops around the gorge and returns to the west side of Midgley Bridge, across the bridge from the trailhead.) Return to the trail fork and continue up the floor of Wilson Canyon. Past the old bridge, the trail narrows to a footpath and follows the streambed up the east side of the canyon floor. At a half mile is a second trail on the right leading up to Wilson Mountain. Eighty yards ahead is a junction on the left with the Jim Thompson Trail (Hike 24) and the Red Rock–Secret Mountain Wilderness boundary near the east tip of Steamboat Rock. Continue up canyon beneath towering Wilson Mountain. The canyon narrows and the trail dances and weaves from side to side along huge, sloping red rock slabs. The trail ends by some of the large rock slabs. About 200 yards before the trail ends, a side path on the right climbs a hill to a canyon overlook.

Hike 14
Wilson Mountain—Wilson Canyon Loop
OAK CREEK CANYON • WILSON CANYON

Hiking distance: 1.5 mile loop
Hiking time: 1 hour
Elevation gain: 300 feet
Maps: U.S.G.S. Munds Park
      Beartooth Publishing—Sedona, AZ

map
next page

Summary of hike: This short loop hike begins and ends on the east side of Midgley Bridge at the mouth of Wilson Canyon. The first part of the hike follows the Wilson Mountain Trail (Hike 11) to elevated views into Wilson Canyon and across to the Schnebly Hill formations. The trail loops down and around into lush Wilson Canyon (Hike 13), following the shaded streambed through rock grottos. Part of the hike follows the old Oak Creek Canyon road, used before Midgley Bridge was built.

Driving directions: From the Sedona Y (Highways 89A and 179 junction), drive 1.9 miles north on Highway 89A (towards Flagstaff) to the parking lot on the left, just after crossing Midgley Bridge.

Hiking directions: Walk up the canyon 20 yards, passing the trailhead map to a junction by the picnic tables. The left fork, straight ahead, is the return route. It leads up the floor of Wilson Canyon (Hike 13). Bear right, heading up the hillside on the east side of the canyon. Follow the red rock path through a mixed forest, overlooking Wilson Canyon, the old highway looping around Wilson Canyon before Midgley Bridge was built, and across Oak Creek Canyon to the Schnebly Hill formations. The path levels out for a long stretch, passing under two sets of power lines, and heads due north towards the flat-topped First Bench of Wilson Mountain. At 0.75 miles is a posted junction at the Red Rock–Secret Mountain Wilderness boundary. The right fork enters the wilderness and climbs Wilson Mountain to the First Bench (Hike 11). Bear left (outside the wilderness boundary) and descend into forested Wilson Canyon beneath steep canyon walls, spires, and pillars. Curve south on the rocky footpath as the grade steepens, reaching the canyon floor and the Wilson Canyon Trail at two metal-encased cairns. The right fork heads deeper into the canyon (Hike 13). Bear left and and head down canyon along the east side of the canyon floor. Pass the remnants of the old Wilson Canyon Bridge as the trail widens. Complete the loop and return to the trailhead by Midgley Bridge.

MIDGLEY
BRIDGE

HIKE 13
WILSON CANYON
HIKE 14
WILSON MOUNTAIN–
WILSON CANYON LOOP

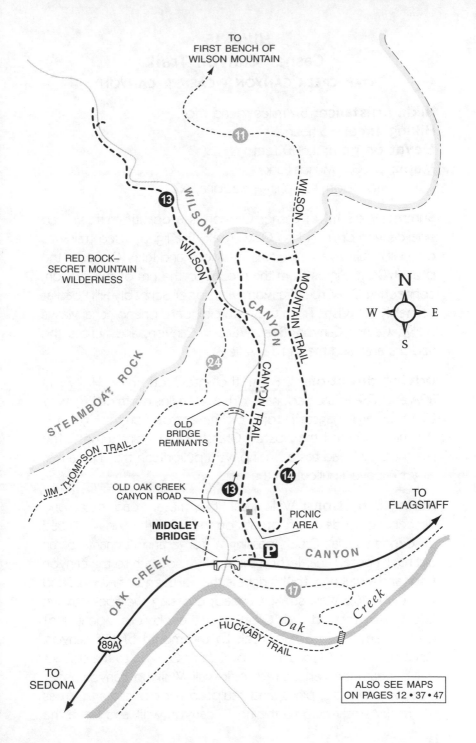

TO
FIRST BENCH OF
WILSON MOUNTAIN

11

WILSON

13

WILSON

WILSON

RED ROCK–
SECRET MOUNTAIN
WILDERNESS

CANYON

MOUNTAIN TRAIL

N
W   E
S

24

CANYON TRAIL

STEAMBOAT ROCK

OLD
BRIDGE
REMNANTS

JIM THOMPSON TRAIL

14

OLD OAK CREEK
CANYON ROAD

13

TO
FLAGSTAFF

PICNIC
AREA

MIDGLEY
BRIDGE

P

CANYON

OAK CREEK

17

Creek

Oak

89A

HUCKABY TRAIL

TO
SEDONA

ALSO SEE MAPS
ON PAGES 12 • 37 • 47

Hike 15
Casner Canyon Trail
OAK CREEK CANYON · CASNER CANYON

Hiking distance: 5.2 miles round trip
Hiking time: 3.5 hours
Elevation gain: 1,600 feet
Maps: U.S.G.S. Munds Park
Beartooth Publishing—Sedona, AZ

Summary of hike: Casner Canyon is a beautiful stream-fed side canyon draining into Oak Creek. The lightly used trail was originally built as a cattle trail by Mose and Riley Casner in the late 1870s. It climbs from the mouth to the rim of the canyon, connecting Oak Creek Canyon with upper Schnebly Hill Road at Schnebly Hill Vista. From the vista point are phenomenal views down Casner Canyon, Bear Wallow Canyon, and across the Sedona area and the Verde Valley.

Driving directions: From the intersection of Highways 89A and 179, at the Sedona Y, drive 2.9 miles north on Highway 89A (towards Flagstaff) to an old gated road on the right. It is 0.4 miles beyond the posted Grasshopper Point turnoff. The unsigned trailhead has a small paved pullout on the right and a larger unpaved pullout on the left.

Hiking directions: Walk past the metal road gate, and descend 15 yards to a footpath on the left. (The unpaved road descends to Oak Creek, passing a gorge and remnants of an old rock house.) Bear left on the rocky footpath to the canyon floor and a trail sign. To the right is the north end of Allen's Bend Trail (Hike 16). Walk straight ahead, crossing the rock-strewn flood plain toward Oak Creek and the obvious opening of Casner Canyon. Ford the creek to the mouth of the canyon. Climb up the right (south) side of Casner Canyon to the distinct trail beneath the vertical red rock wall. Walk up-canyon under a canopy of oaks, pines, and sculpted rock overhangs. Cross the rocky streambed to the north canyon wall, and leave the pine and cypress forest to the exposed chaparral and cactus covering the hillside. As the elevation increases, views open to upper Casner Canyon and across West Sedona. At 1.2 miles, the trail curves left (northeast) into the north fork of the canyon, beneath Indian Point. Begin climbing in earnest to the base of the jagged canyon wall. Curve east and climb through pockets of dense brush. The canyon narrows to the notch in the mountains at the summit. Pass through an old wooden gate, and leave the canyon on a gentle uphill grade. Cross the open mountaintop dotted with juniper and head south. Cairns mark the route as the trail fades in and out. Pass through two consecutive barbed wire gates to the parking area at Schnebly Hill Vista.

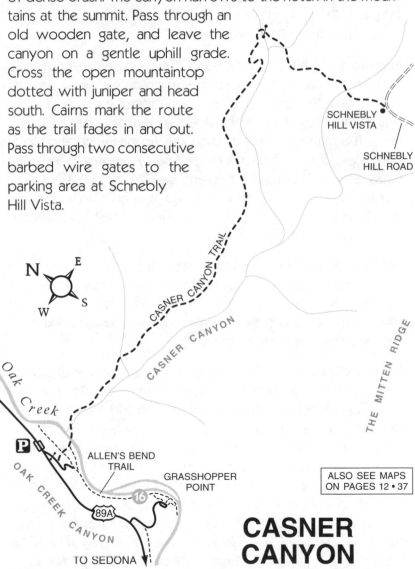

SCHNEBLY HILL VISTA

SCHNEBLY HILL ROAD

THE MITTEN RIDGE

CASNER CANYON TRAIL

CASNER CANYON

CASNER CANYON

Oak Creek

P

ALLEN'S BEND TRAIL

GRASSHOPPER POINT

ALSO SEE MAPS ON PAGES 12 • 37

OAK CREEK CANYON

89A

16

TO SEDONA

CASNER CANYON

Hike 16
Allen's Bend Trail and Grasshopper Point
OAK CREEK CANYON

Hiking distance: 1 mile round trip
Hiking time: 30 minutes
Elevation gain: 100 feet
Maps: U.S.G.S. Munds Park
Beartooth Publishing—Sedona, AZ

Summary of hike: Allen's Bend Trail is an easy and scenic creekside walk along a half-mile stretch on the west bank of Oak Creek. The trail starts at Grasshopper Point, a popular swimming hole with large boulders at the base of sandstone cliffs. The path meanders through lush riparian vegetation, pinyon pines, juniper, scrub live oak, a few sycamores, ponderosa pines, and an old orchard. Numerous side paths lead from the red sandstone cliffs to the water's edge, lined with large rocks and deep pools. Watch for an Indian ruin in a small cave near the trail.

Driving directions: From the Sedona Y (Highways 89A and 179 junction), drive 2.5 miles north on Highway 89A (towards Flagstaff) to a posted turnoff on the right for Grasshopper Point. Turn right and drive downhill 0.2 miles to the parking lot below. A parking fee is required.

Hiking directions: From the parking lot, take one of several trails down to Oak Creek. Head downstream (south) to the pool at Grasshopper Point. Return to the north and take the Allen's Bend Trail up canyon. Walk on a ledge along the 100-foot-high west wall of the canyon above Oak Creek. Along the trail are rock pathways, steps, and overhanging cliffs. Several side paths provide access to the creek. Pass a small Indian ruin on the left in a shallow cave. A short distance ahead is the old campground road on the left near the remnants of rock structures. The dirt road ascends the hillside to the highway at the Casner Canyon trailhead (Hike 15). Continue straight ahead to a junction with the Casner Canyon Trail on the right, leading to Oak Creek at the mouth of Casner Canyon. Beyond the junction are more pools along the creek. Return by retracing your steps.

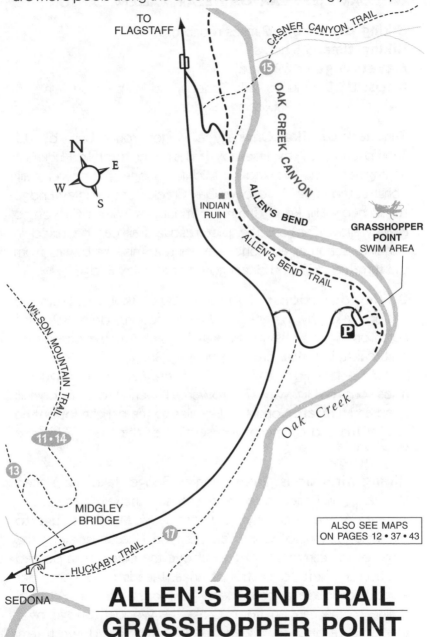

TO FLAGSTAFF

CASNER CANYON TRAIL

15

OAK CREEK CANYON

N
E
W
S

INDIAN RUIN

ALLEN'S BEND

ALLEN'S BEND TRAIL

GRASSHOPPER POINT
SWIM AREA

P

WILSON MOUNTAIN TRAIL

Oak Creek

11·14

13

MIDGLEY BRIDGE

17

HUCKABY TRAIL

ALSO SEE MAPS
ON PAGES 12 • 37 • 43

TO SEDONA

ALLEN'S BEND TRAIL
GRASSHOPPER POINT

Hike 17
Huckaby Trail from Midgley Bridge
OAK CREEK CANYON · BEAR WALLOW CANYON

Hiking distance: 5.2 miles round trip
Hiking time: 2.5 hours
Elevation gain: 500 feet
Maps: U.S.G.S. Munds Park, Sedona, and Munds Mountain
       Beartooth Publishing—Sedona, AZ

Summary of hike: Originally a wagon route built by J.J. Thompson in 1887, the Huckaby Trail is named after Jim Huckaby, an engineer who worked on Midgley Bridge. The newer trail, constructed in 1998, follows Oak Creek from Midgley Bridge to Schnebly Hill Road, from the mouth of Wilson Canyon to Bear Wallow Canyon. The picturesque trail can be hiked in either direction or as a one-way shuttle. This hike begins from the turreted cliffs and deep gorge at Midgley Bridge.

Driving directions: To MIDGLEY BRIDGE TRAILHEAD: From the Sedona Y (Highways 89A and 179 junction), drive 1.9 miles north on Highway 89A (towards Flagstaff) to the parking lot on the left, just after crossing Midgley Bridge.

To SCHNEBLY HILL TRAILHEAD: From the Sedona Y, drive 0.3 miles south on Highway 179 (towards Phoenix) to Schnebly Hill Road and turn left. Continue 0.9 miles to the parking lot on the left, at the end of the paved section of the road. (Also see Hike 18.)

Hiking directions: From Midgley Bridge, take the signed Huckaby Trail. Descend red rock steps to the railing and viewing area of the two canyons. Cross under Midgley Bridge to the vista lookout of Oak Creek Canyon. Head east along the edge of the canyon, 200 feet above the creek, to a posted junction. The left fork (straight ahead) leads to Grasshopper Point (Hike 16). Take the Huckaby Trail to the right on a gradual incline to the canyon floor. Cross the wooden bridge over Oak Creek, and follow the east bank of the creek downstream.

Cross another bridge over a branch of Oak Creek. Traverse the east canyon wall on a rock shelf, passing a series of pools. At 1.2 miles make a horseshoe left bend. Ascend the canyon wall to views of Wilson Mountain, Uptown Sedona, Cathedral Rock, and a vista filled with red rock formations. Curve in and around a small, forested side canyon on the west-pointing toe of Mitten Ridge. Drop into Bear Wallow Canyon, and follow the contours of the north canyon wall, zigzagging to an overlook with a bench. Wind down to the canyon floor, and climb out of the red rock wash to the south side on a plateau near Schnebly Hill Road and a posted junction. The right fork leads to the road and Marg's Draw (Hike 77). The left fork (straight ahead) leads up canyon to the trailhead parking lot for Marg's Draw and Munds Wagon Trail.

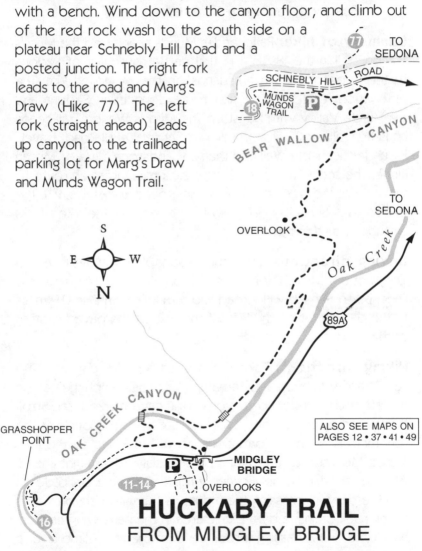

ALSO SEE MAPS ON
PAGES 12 • 37 • 41 • 49

HUCKABY TRAIL
FROM MIDGLEY BRIDGE

Hike 18
Munds Wagon Trail
SCHNEBLY HILL ROAD

Hiking distance: 8 miles round trip

Hiking time: 4 hours

Elevation gain: 1,200 feet

Maps: U.S.G.S. Sedona, Munds Mountain, and Munds Park
  Beartooth Publishing—Sedona, AZ

map
page 52

Summary of hike: Rancher Jim Munds pioneered the Munds Wagon Trail in the 1890s, the first cattle route out of Sedona to the upper mountain grasslands on the Mogollon Rim. The old wagon road was the first route connecting Sedona and the Verde Valley with Flagstaff. The Munds Wagon Trail heads up Bear Wallow Canyon parallel to Schnebly Hill Road, traveling under Schnebly Wall and the red sandstone cliffs of Mitten Ridge. The scenic trail passes large slick rock areas en route to the head of the canyon at Merry-Go-Round Rock (Hike 21). The trail crosses Schnebly Hill Road four times, yet the hike offers solitude and stunning visuals.

Driving directions: From the Sedona Y (Highways 89A and 179 junction), drive 0.3 miles south on Highway 179 (towards Phoenix) to Schnebly Hill Road and turn left. Continue 0.9 miles to the parking lot on the left, at the end of the paved section of the road.

Hiking directions: Take the posted red dirt path east up Bear Wallow Canyon. Pass a natural red rock amphitheater on the left, and meander up canyon on the cairn-marked trail. Stroll through an open Arizona cypress forest, surrounded by the spectacular red rock formations of Mitten Ridge to the left, Munds Mountain to the right, and Schnebly Hill straight ahead. At a quarter mile, cross Schnebly Hill Road twice. Drop down into the canyon, crossing the mouth of Damfino Canyon. Cross a slick rock drainage by a picnic area in the narrowing canyon. Walk up a draw, passing a rock cave on the left. Climb over a hill, dropping into a forested draw at the base of the towering vertical red rock wall of Mitten Ridge. Follow the south flank of the sculpted formation, which soon curves away to the north. The trail steadily dips and rises up a narrow slab rock channel. Zigzag uphill and cross Schnebly Hill Road at 2.5 miles to a junction with the Cow Pies Trail (Hikes 19 and 20). Stay to the right and cross the road for the fourth and final time. Curve left, directly toward Merry-Go-Round Rock (Hike 21). At the corner of Merry-Go-Round Rock, on a ledge midway up the formation, is a junction. The right fork ends at Schnebly Hill Road. The left fork circles the Merry-Go-Round clockwise to overlooks of the entire canyon. Continue past the formation, and cross the head of Bear Wallow Canyon to the end of the trail at Schnebly Hill Road at the Schnebly Hill Trailhead (Hike 22).

Hike 19
Cow Pies
SCHNEBLY HILL ROAD

Hiking distance: 3 miles round trip
Hiking time: 1.5 hours
Elevation gain: 100 feet
Maps: U.S.G.S. Munds Mountain and Munds Park
Beartooth Publishing—Sedona, AZ

map
page 52

Summary of hike: The Cow Pies are multilevel, flat red rock mounds located in the middle of Bear Wallow Canyon. From the edge of the enormous slick rock mounds are world-class views into the canyon below. The circular sandstone formations are one of Sedona's foremost vortex sites. Stones carefully placed in a circle, known as medicine wheels, are used as an antenna to attract positive energies. Medicine wheels are usually seen on the upper Cow Pies. Various pathways lead from one mound formation to the next. John Wayne was filmed at this site while acting in the 1940s film Angel and the Badman.

Driving directions: From the Sedona Y (Highways 89A and 179 junction), drive 0.3 miles south on Highway 179 (towards Phoenix) to Schnebly Hill Road and turn left. Continue 3.6 miles on the rough, unpaved road to the trailhead parking area on the right.

Hiking directions: From this trailhead, the Munds Wagon Trail heads east to the head of Bear Wallow Canyon and west down canyon towards Sedona (Hike 18). Cross the road to the signed Cow Pies Trail and head north. The red rock path descends into Bear Wallow Canyon directly toward Mitten Ridge, with Merry-Go-Round Rock and Schnebly Hill to the east (right). Enter the cypress forest and cross a streambed to a large, red slick rock shelf. A medicine wheel frequently lies on this site. Cross the rock shelf and ascend a second rock shelf to a trail junction at a half mile. Mitten Ridge (Hike 20) is straight ahead on the right fork. Bear left and head west toward the Cow Pies. Paths lead from one large mound to another, each one as amazing as the last. The substantial scale and height of the circular formations is realized along the west edges of the rock mounds. Follow the various pathways, exploring along your own route.

Hike 20
Mitten Ridge
SCHNEBLY HILL ROAD

Hiking distance: 3 to 5 miles round trip
Hiking time: 2.5 hours
Elevation gain: 300 feet
Maps: U.S.G.S. Munds Mountain and Munds Park
Beartooth Publishing—Sedona, AZ

map
next page

Summary of hike: Mitten Ridge is a long band of weathered, jagged red rock formations forming the north wall of Bear Wallow Canyon. The terra cotta sandstone cliffs are sculpted into fantastic shapes with columns, caves, overhangs, and buttes. The trail follows the contours along the base of Mitten Ridge, offering close-up views of the scenic canyon and its awesome formations.

Driving directions: From the Sedona Y (Highways 89A and 179 junction), drive 0.3 miles south on Highway 179 (towards Phoenix) to Schnebly Hill Road and turn left. Continue 3.6 miles on the rough, unpaved road to the trailhead parking area on the right.

Hiking directions: From this trailhead, the Munds Wagon Trail heads east to the head of Bear Wallow Canyon and west down canyon towards Sedona (Hike 18). Cross the road to the signed Cow Pies Trail and head north. The red rock path descends into Bear Wallow Canyon directly toward Mitten Ridge, with Merry-Go-Round Rock and Schnebly Hill to the east (right). Enter the cypress forest and cross a streambed to a large, red slick rock shelf. This area is considered a power center and is often the site of large medicine wheels—stones placed in a circle to draw in positive spiritual energies. Cross the rock shelf and ascend a second rock shelf to a trail junction at a half mile. The Cow Pies Trail (Hike 19) bears left and heads west through the middle of Bear Wallow Canyon. Continue straight and head north toward weather-carved Mitten Ridge. Cairns mark the route to the base of the red sandstone cliffs. At the base, trails lead in both directions. Follow your own route, exploring the crevices, caves, and higher ledges of the sculpted landscape. Use caution negotiating your way up to the various shelves, landings, and buttes. The pristine open area allows easy exploration without getting lost. Return along the same route.

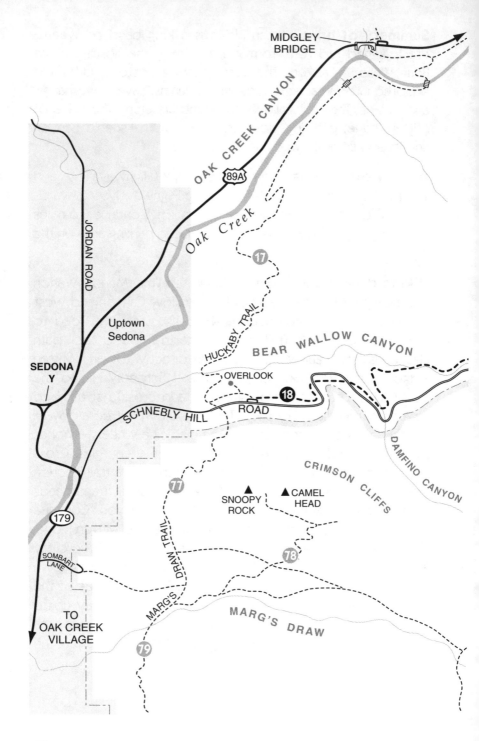

MIDGLEY
BRIDGE

OAK CREEK CANYON

89A

Oak Creek

JORDAN ROAD

Uptown
Sedona

17

HUCKABY TRAIL

BEAR WALLOW CANYON

SEDONA
Y

OVERLOOK

SCHNEBLY HILL ROAD 18

DAMFINO CANYON

179

77

CRIMSON CLIFFS

▲
SNOOPY
ROCK

▲ CAMEL
HEAD

SOMBART
LANE

78

MARG'S DRAW TRAIL

TO
OAK CREEK
VILLAGE

MARG'S DRAW

79

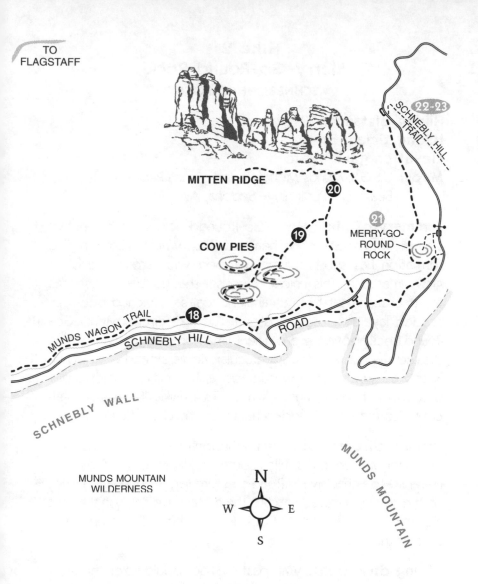

TO
FLAGSTAFF

22-23

SCHNEBLY HILL TRAIL

MITTEN RIDGE

20

21

COW PIES

19

MERRY-GO-
ROUND
ROCK

MUNDS WAGON TRAIL

18

SCHNEBLY HILL ROAD

SCHNEBLY WALL

MUNDS MOUNTAIN
WILDERNESS

N
W E
S

MUNDS MOUNTAIN

HIKE 18
MUNDS WAGON TRAIL
HIKES 19 • 20
COW PIES • MITTEN RIDGE
SCHNEBLY HILL ROAD

Hike 21
Merry-Go-Round Rock
SCHNEBLY HILL ROAD

Hiking distance: 1.2 mile loop
Hiking time: 45 minutes
Elevation gain: 100 feet
Maps: U.S.G.S. Munds Mountain and Munds Park
Beartooth Publishing—Sedona, AZ

Summary of hike: Merry-Go-Round Rock is the distinctive circular formation at the head of Bear Wallow Canyon. The formation has short columns capped with erosion-resistant grey limestone. This unique carousel-shaped band illustrates the encroachment from an ancient sea, sandwiched between eroded layers of red sandstone. This hike circles Merry-Go-Round Rock above the prominent limestone ledge, overlooking the red sandstone cliffs. Spectacular views extend west down Bear Wallow Canyon toward Sedona. The ledge was originally part of the historic Munds Wagon Trail (Hike 18). A side path climbs to the summit, adding height to the dramatic vistas.

Driving directions: From the Sedona Y (Highways 89A and 179 junction), drive 0.3 miles south on Highway 179 (towards Phoenix) to Schnebly Hill Road and turn left. Continue 4.6 miles on the rough, unpaved road to the metal pipe gate on the east side of Merry-Go-Round Rock. Park in the pullouts on either side of the road.

Hiking directions: Walk past the rock boulders on the west side of the road toward Merry-Go-Round Rock and a trail fork. Take the right fork straight ahead to the summit and panoramic overlooks. From the overlooks are vistas down Bear Wallow Canyon of Mitten Ridge, the Cow Pies, Munds Mountain, and Sedona. Return to the junction and take the unsigned south fork. Descend along the base of the formation 70 yards to a posted junction with the Munds Wagon Trail (Hike 18). Take the right fork and curve around the south and west sides of Merry-Go-

Round Rock on an elevated platform mid-way up the formation. Curve north through a forest of Arizona cypress, away from the Merry-Go-Round. Cross the head of Bear Wallow Canyon, and gently climb parallel and below Schnebly Hill Road. The trail ends at the road, across from the Schnebly Hill Trail (Hike 22). Retrace your steps or return down Schnebly Hill Road.

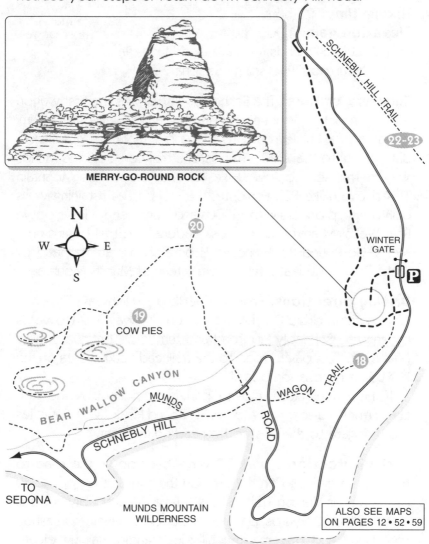

MERRY-GO-ROUND ROCK

MERRY-GO-ROUND ROCK

Hike 22
Schnebly Hill Trail
SCHNEBLY HILL ROAD

Hiking distance: 4.8 miles round trip
             (plus 0.8 miles if winter gate is closed)
Hiking time: 2.5 hours
Elevation gain: 1,000 feet

map
next page

Maps: U.S.G.S. Munds Mountain and Munds Park
     Beartooth Publishing—Sedona, AZ

Summary of hike: The Schnebly Hill Trail was the first wagon route connecting Sedona with Flagstaff atop the Mogollon Rim. It was also a cattle route to the upper mountain grasslands, dating back to the 1890s. The historic trail connects the Munds Wagon Trail seen below (Hike 18) with the Munds Mountain Trail above (Hike 23). En route, the trail passes retaining walls built by the pioneers in the 1800s and magnificent views down Bear Wallow Canyon and across Sedona. The trail begins near Merry-Go-Round Rock and ends on a saddle at the head of Jacks Canyon beneath the upper plateau of Munds Mountain.

Driving directions: From the Sedona Y (Highways 89A and 179 junction), drive 0.3 miles south on Highway 179 (towards Phoenix) to Schnebly Hill Road and turn left. Continue 5 miles on the rough, unpaved road to the trailhead parking area on the left by an information board.

If the winter gate is closed, park in the pullout by the gate at 4.6 miles, adjacent to Merry-Go-Round Rock. Walk 0.4 miles past the gate to the posted trailhead on the right.

Hiking directions: Walk 80 yards back down the road to the posted trailhead on the left. On the right is the upper end of the Munds Wagon Trail (Hike 18). Take the Schnebly Hill Trail up the hillside 80 yards, parallel to the road. Make a horseshoe right bend and traverse the hillside, steadily gaining elevation on the former wagon road. Spectacular bird's-eye views extend down Bear Wallow Canyon, with the Schnebly Hill Road

56 - Day Hikes Around Sedona

snaking downward. The views stretch across the Sedona–Verde Valley corridor to Cottonwood, Jerome, and the Black Hills. At the top of the grade, on the Mogollon Rim, the wagon road curves left and heads north. Leave the road and take the posted trail, veering to the right. The cairn-marked path weaves through a pine forest perched on the cliffs. Cross a minor draw and pass through a cattle gate. Pass through a second gate to an open plateau dotted with juniper and a great view of Sedona. Detour left, leaving the main trail to Committee Tank, a circular cattle pond built up with a dirt mound. Back on the trail, cross the plateau to the head of forested Jacks Canyon. Drop down to a saddle with the Hot Loop Trail coming in from the left (Hike 98). Continue straight ahead for 80 yards to the end of the Schnebly Hill Trail at a Y-fork on Munds Saddle. The Jacks Canyon Trail (Hike 97) steeply descends en route to the Village of Oak Creek. The Munds Mountain Trail (Hike 23) continues on the right fork. Return by retracing your steps.

Hike 23
Munds Mountain Trail
SCHNEBLY HILL ROAD

Hiking distance: 9.6 miles round trip
(plus 0.8 miles if winter gate is closed)
Hiking time: 5 hours
Elevation gain: 1,400 feet

map
next page

Maps: U.S.G.S. Munds Mountain and Munds Park
Beartooth Publishing—Sedona, AZ

Summary of hike: Munds Mountain is the enormous 6,834-foot mountain that forms the east boundary of Sedona, running parallel to Highway 179. The towering mountain resides between Schnebly Hill and Lee Mountain and is entirely within the 18,150-acre Munds Mountain Wilderness. There are three access routes to the vast upper plateau. This hike follows the shortest and easiest route from Schnebley Hill Road. The Munds Mountain Trail begins on the saddle at the head of Jacks

Canyon and climbs the northeast slope to the isolated and scenic plateau.

Driving directions: Same as Hike 22.

Hiking directions: Follow the Schnebly Hill Trail hiking directions (Hike 22) to Munds Saddle at the head of Jacks Canyon. From the Munds Mountain–Jacks Canyon junction at Munds Saddle, continue straight ahead on the right fork. Climb up the east flank of Munds Mountain on a rock and sand path. The cairn-marked trail zigzags up the edge of the mountain to a narrow ridge straddling Jacks Canyon and Bear Wallow Canyon. Follow the ridge south and begin a second steep climb to the 6,834-foot plateau. Cross the open grasslands with scattered junipers and head south. From the north and west edge of the expansive plateau are vistas of the hiking route just taken, lower Oak Creek Canyon, and Sedona. The main trail crosses through the middle of the plateau and gently slopes downhill for 300 feet to views of Cathedral Rock. Follow the cairns as the trail fades in and out to a large meadow near the south rim, overlooking Lee Mountain and Jacks Canyon. At this point there are more animal tracks than shoe prints. Return along the same route.

HIKE 22
SCHNEBLY HILL TRAIL

HIKE 23
MUNDS MOUNTAIN TRAIL
SCHNEBLY HILL ROAD

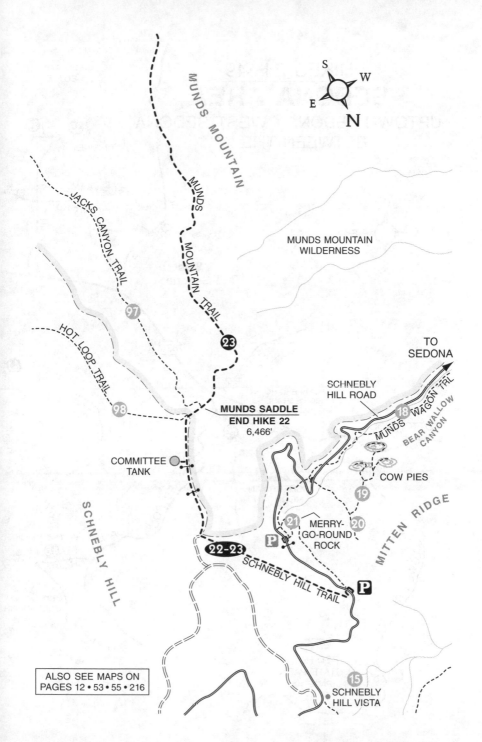

MUNDS MOUNTAIN

MUNDS MOUNTAIN TRAIL

JACKS CANYON TRAIL

HOT LOOP TRAIL

97

98

23

MUNDS MOUNTAIN
WILDERNESS

TO
SEDONA

SCHNEBLY
HILL ROAD

MUNDS WAGON TRL

BEAR WALLOW CANYON

18

MUNDS SADDLE
END HIKE 22
6,466'

COMMITTEE
TANK

COW PIES

19

20

21

MERRY-
GO-ROUND
ROCK

MITTEN RIDGE

SCHNEBLY HILL

22-23

P

P

SCHNEBLY HILL TRAIL

ALSO SEE MAPS ON
PAGES 12 • 53 • 55 • 216

15

SCHNEBLY
HILL VISTA

100 Great Hikes – **59**

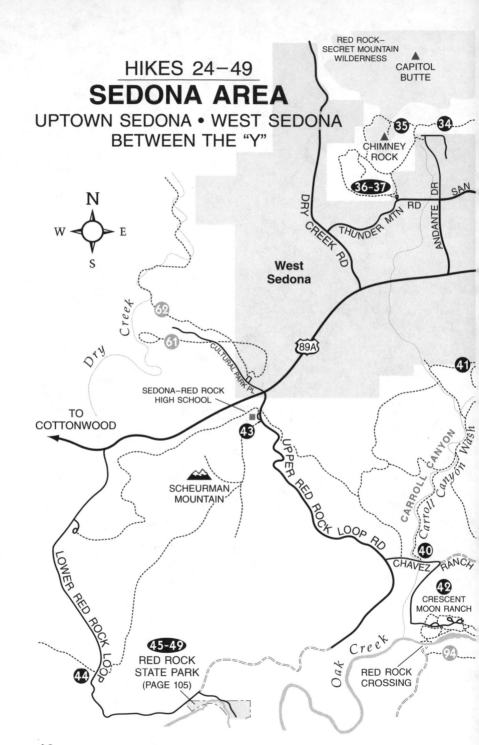

HIKES 24–49
SEDONA AREA
UPTOWN SEDONA • WEST SEDONA
BETWEEN THE "Y"

RED ROCK–
SECRET MOUNTAIN
WILDERNESS
▲ CAPITOL
BUTTE

35 34

CHIMNEY
ROCK

36-37

DRY CREEK RD

THUNDER MTN RD

ANDANTE DR

SAN

N
W   E
S

West
Sedona

Creek

62

Dry

61

CULTURAL PARK PL

89A

41

SEDONA–RED ROCK
HIGH SCHOOL

TO
COTTONWOOD

43

UPPER RED ROCK LOOP RD

SCHEURMAN
MOUNTAIN

CARROLL CANYON

Carroll Canyon Wash

40

CHAVEZ RANCH

42
CRESCENT
MOON RANCH

LOWER RED ROCK LOOP

Creek

Oak

94

44

45-49
RED ROCK
STATE PARK
(PAGE 105)

RED ROCK
CROSSING

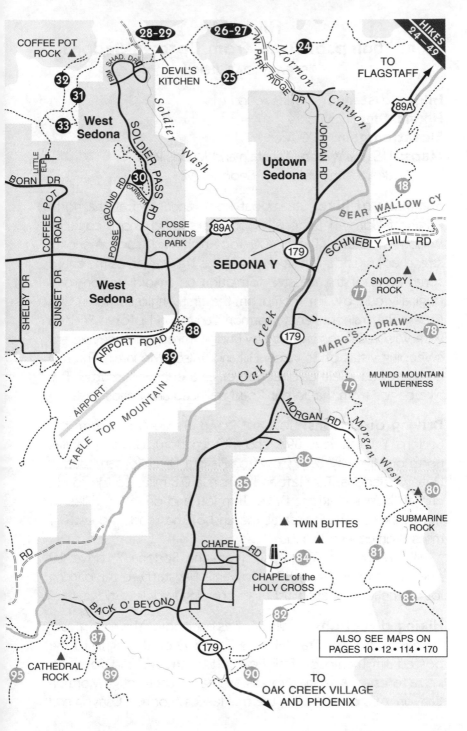

Hike 24
Jim Thompson Trail from Uptown Sedona
STEAMBOAT ROCK

Hiking distance: 5 miles round trip
Hiking time: 2.5 hours
Elevation gain: 400 feet
Maps: U.S.G.S. Wilson Mountain and Munds Park
Beartooth Publishing—Sedona, AZ

Summary of hike: Steamboat Rock, anchored at the north edge of Uptown Sedona, is on the southernmost edge of Wilson Mountain. The 5,400-foot-high red rock monolith stretches just under a mile in length. This trail traverses the entire south edge of the massive formation on an old wagon road originally built by Jim Thompson, the first Anglo settler in Oak Creek. The trail connects Mormon Canyon in Uptown Sedona with Wilson Canyon by Midgley Bridge. Throughout the hike are sweeping vistas of Schnebly Hill and Wilson Mountain. The trail can be hiked in either direction or as a one-way shuttle. This hike begins from the Jordan Road trailhead and heads east.

Driving directions: JORDAN ROAD TRAILHEAD: From the Sedona Y (Highways 89A and 179 junction), drive 0.3 miles north on Highway 89A (towards Flagstaff) to Jordan Road in Uptown Sedona. Turn left and continue 0.8 miles to the road's end at West Park Ridge Drive. Turn left and drive 0.6 miles to the trailhead parking area at the end of the road. The last 0.4 miles is on unpaved road.

MIDGLEY BRIDGE TRAILHEAD: From the Sedona Y, drive 1.9 miles north on Highway 89A (towards Flagstaff) to the parking lot on the left, located just after crossing Midgley Bridge.

Hiking directions: Walk 0.1 miles back down the road, passing the Cibola Pass Trail (Hikes 25 and 27) on the right, to the posted Jim Thompson Trail. Bear left on the red dirt footpath into a forest of Arizona cypress, and head east through Mormon Canyon. At a quarter mile, the trail leaves Mormon Canyon and gains elevation, with views of the sculpted south rim of Wilson Mountain. Pass through a cattle gate, and head directly toward the southeast end of Steamboat Rock. Curve north on the wide, rocky path. Loop around the forested canyon to the base of Steamboat Rock. Curve around the west tip of Steamboat Rock, and traverse the hillside cliff along the south flank of the massive formation. At the east end, descend into Wilson Canyon. The rocky cliffside path steadily drops along the west wall of the forested canyon. The trail ends at a posted junction on the floor of Wilson Canyon at the Red Rock–Secret Mountain Wilderness boundary. The left fork heads farther into Wilson Canyon (Hike 13). The right fork leads 0.6 miles to Midgley Bridge. Return by retracing your route.

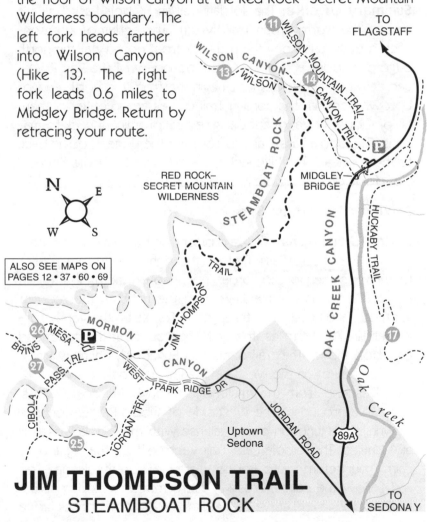

ALSO SEE MAPS ON
PAGES 12 • 37 • 60 • 69

JIM THOMPSON TRAIL
STEAMBOAT ROCK

Hike 25
Jordan Trail—Devil's Kitchen—
Cibola Pass Loop

Hiking distance: 2.5 mile loop
Hiking time: 1.5 hours
Elevation gain: 200 feet
Maps: U.S.G.S. Wilson Mountain
Beartooth Publishing—Sedona, AZ

Summary of hike: The Jordan Trail and Cibola Pass Trail are part of the North Urban Trail System. This series of interconnected trails runs along the red rock front country at the north edge of Sedona and the southern boundary of the Red Rock–Secret Mountain Wilderness. Beginning from the north end of Uptown Sedona, the Jordan Trail curves around the southern tip of Cibola Ridge, overlooking several prominent rock formations. The Cibola Pass Trail crosses over the ridge, looping back to the trailhead. The hike includes a side trip to Devil's Kitchen, a 65-foot-deep sinkhole in Soldier Wash.

Driving directions: Same as Hike 26.

Hiking directions: Walk a quarter mile back down the road, passing the Cibola Pass Trail on the right (the return route). Continue to the posted Jordan Trail, also on the right, located at a left bend in the road. Veer to the right on the red dirt footpath, and head west through the forest on the gently rolling terrain. At 0.4 miles, the path tops out near the south end of Cibola Ridge. The trail overlooks Sugarloaf, Chimney Rock, and Coffee Pot to the west and Steamboat Rock to the northeast. Descend from the small ridge through Arizona cypress, and curve around to the west side of Cibola Ridge. Continue downhill to a junction on a small rise with the Cibola Pass Trail at 1.1 miles. The Cibola Pass Trail veers off to the right by a cairn—our return route. For now, stay left on the Jordan Trail and follow the cairns, crossing a streambed. Walk across the red rock ledge and curve to the right. Cross another rock ledge to a junction with the Soldier Pass Trail (Hikes 28 and 29). Curve to the right 30 yards to the Devil's Kitchen sinkhole on the right.

Return a quarter mile to the junction with the Cibola Pass Trail. Take the left fork and head east, meandering through the cypress forest beneath the sculpted spires. Ascend Cibola Ridge to an overlook. Pass through a trail gate on the summit and go to the right. Zigzag down the east side of the ridge, completing the loop on the dirt road. Return to the left.

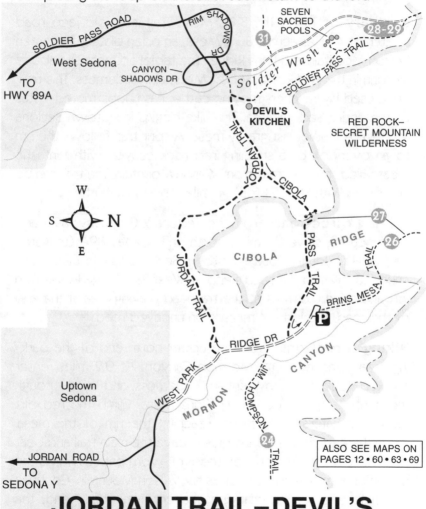

JORDAN TRAIL–DEVIL'S KITCHEN–CIBOLA PASS

Hike 26
Brins Mesa Trail from Uptown Sedona

Hiking distance: 6 miles round trip
Hiking time: 3 hours
Elevation gain: 700 feet
Maps: U.S.G.S. Wilson Mountain
　　　　Beartooth Publishing—Sedona, AZ

map
next page

Summary of hike: The Brins Mesa Trail is an old jeep road stretching 4 miles across Brins Mesa, an open plateau between Wilson Mountain and Brins Ridge. The tabletop mesa sits above Sedona in the Red Rock—Secret Mountain Wilderness. This trail, once used by ranchers moving cattle, has unobstructed vistas of the entire Sedona area. The hike begins in Uptown Sedona and climbs to the vast grassy mesa. A spur trail follows the rim to an overlook of a stunning red rock canyon with fantastic weathered spires across from Wilson Mountain. The trail can be combined with Hike 53 for a 4-mile, one-way shuttle.

Driving directions: From the Sedona Y (Highways 89A and 179 junction), drive 0.3 miles north on Highway 89A (towards Flagstaff) to Jordan Road in Uptown Sedona. Turn left and continue 0.8 miles to the road's end at West Park Ridge Drive. Turn left and drive 0.6 miles to the trailhead parking area at the end of the road. The last 0.4 miles is on unpaved road.

Hiking directions: From the upper north end of the parking area, head north up Mormon Canyon. At 0.2 miles, enter the Red Rock—Secret Mountain Wilderness, and wind through the gently sloping foothills of Brins Mesa. Climb the red dirt path with natural rock steps, reaching the rim of the mesa. Atop the east ridge of Brins Mesa, leave the main trail and bear right. Follow the rim north on the well-worn path towards the magnificent multi-colored spires by Wilson Mountain. Continue one mile through the changing scenery. Near trail's end, the path fades. Stay close to the rim at a deep chasm across from

Wilson Mountain. Return to the Brins Mesa Trail, and head back along the same path.

To extend the hike, continue northwest on the Brins Mesa Trail, crossing the plateau to a junction with the Soldier Pass Trail (Hike 29). The left fork crosses over the rise to Soldier Pass and descends the canyon to Seven Sacred Pools and Devil's Kitchen. The Brins Mesa Trail continues 2 miles northwest to the parking area on Dry Creek Road (Hike 53).

Hike 27
Cibola Pass—Soldier Pass—Brins Mesa Loop

Hiking distance: 5.5 mile loop
Hiking time: 3 hours
Elevation gain: 700 feet
Maps: U.S.G.S. Wilson Mountain
      Beartooth Publishing—Sedona, AZ

*map
next page*

Summary of hike: This loop hike just north of Sedona combines three trails and a variety of scenery. The hike climbs over the 100-foot Cibola Pass and descends to the mouth of Soldier Wash. The Soldier Pass Trail climbs the wash, passing the Devil's Kitchen and Seven Sacred Pools. The area has a series of descending pools etched into the rock, usually filled with snowmelt and rain water. At the head of the canyon, the path crosses over Soldier Pass to Brins Mesa, an open plateau 800 feet above Sedona. The hike returns by crossing the plateau and descending into Mormon Canyon.

Driving directions: Same as Hike 26.

Hiking directions: Walk 100 yards back down the road to the posted Cibola Pass Trail on the right. Take the red dirt footpath into the forest, and climb to the ridge on Cibola Pass, enjoying the sweeping vistas. Follow the ridge 15 yards to the right to a fence gate on the left. Pass through the gate and descend the west-facing slope to the canyon bottom.

At 0.8 miles, just before reaching the canyon floor, the Cibola Pass Trail merges with the Jordan Trail coming in from the left (Hike 25). Continue to the right on the Jordan Trail, crossing a streambed. Walk across the red rock ledge and curve to the right. Cross another rock ledge to a junction with the Soldier Pass Trail (Hikes 28 and 29). The left fork returns to the Soldier Pass trailhead. Curve to the right 30 yards to the Devil's Kitchen, a 65-foot sinkhole. Head north up the canyon 100 yards to a junction with the Teacup Trail on the left (Hike 31). Stay to the right, weaving across red dirt and red slab rock through an open forest. Dramatic red rock formations surround the trail. Follow the east wall of the canyon through eroding sedimentary formations to a flat slick rock area on the left at Seven Sacred Pools. After exploring the pools, continue along the trail located behind the pools to the east. Wind through the forest along the contours of the hillside to the posted wilderness boundary by the streambed at the far end of the jeep access road. Pass the boundary gate and walk up the canyon floor to a Y-fork. The right fork leads to the Soldier Pass Arches (Hike 28). Take the narrower left fork towards Soldier Pass, staying near the canyon bottom. The three arches can be seen on the east canyon wall. Climb to a ridge and follow the ridge north, ascending nearly 400 feet. At the top, the path levels out and crosses Soldier Pass. Descend east to a T-junction with the Brins Mesa Trail. Head to the right (southeast) across the mesa top for a half mile to the edge of the rim overlooking Uptown Sedona, Munds Mountain, Schnebly Hill, and Mitten Ridge. Descend a half mile over natural rock steps and red dirt to the north end of the parking area.

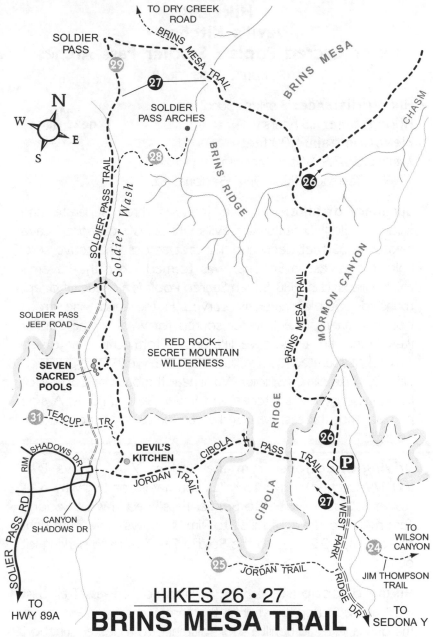

TO DRY CREEK ROAD

SOLDIER PASS

BRINS MESA TRAIL

BRINS MESA

29

27

CHASM

SOLDIER PASS ARCHES

BRINS RIDGE

28

26

N
W E
S

MORMON CANYON

SOLDIER PASS TRAIL

Soldier Wash

BRINS MESA TRAIL

SOLDIER PASS JEEP ROAD

RED ROCK– SECRET MOUNTAIN WILDERNESS

SEVEN SACRED POOLS

CIBOLA PASS TRAIL

26

31 TEACUP TRL

P

DEVIL'S KITCHEN

CIBOLA PASS TRAIL

27

CIBOLA RIDGE

RIM SHADOWS DR

JORDAN TRAIL

SOLDIER PASS RD

WEST PARK RIDGE DR

TO WILSON CANYON

24

CANYON SHADOWS DR

25 JORDAN TRAIL

JIM THOMPSON TRAIL

TO HWY 89A

TO SEDONA Y

HIKES 26 • 27
BRINS MESA TRAIL
CIBOLA PASS–SOLDIER PASS–
BRINS MESA LOOP

Hike 28
Devil's Kitchen •
Seven Sacred Pools • Soldier Pass Arches
SOLDIER PASS TRAIL

Hiking distance: 3 miles round trip
Hiking time: 1.5 hours
Elevation gain: 400 feet
Maps: U.S.G.S. Wilson Mountain
Beartooth Publishing—Sedona, AZ

map next page

Summary of hike: This hike features three separate and unique geological features. Devil's Kitchen is a collapsed cave measuring 65 feet deep and 112 feet across. The active sinkhole, the largest in Sedona, was formed when the cavern's roof collapsed in 1888. Seven Sacred Pools is a queue of deep, rounded potholes naturally carved in the sandstone creek bed. It is an important water source for wildlife. The Soldier Pass Arches are three cave-like arches formed in a large slab of rock, separated by fractures on the west-facing canyon cliff. This hike climbs Soldier Wash near the base of Coffeepot Rock, passing Devil's Kitchen and Seven Sacred Pools. A side path ascends the east wall of the canyon to an overlook at the majestic arches.

Driving directions: From the Sedona Y (Highways 89A and 179 junction), drive 1.3 miles southwest on Highway 89A (towards Cottonwood) to Soldier Pass Road in West Sedona. Turn right and drive 1.4 miles to Rim Shadows Drive. Turn right and continue 0.2 miles to the Soldier Pass Trailhead parking lot on the left.

Hiking directions: Take the posted Soldier Pass Trail past the trail map. Drop down into the forested canyon and cross the drainage. Head uphill a short distance to a posted junction. The Jordan Trail goes to the right, leading to Mormon Canyon above Uptown Sedona (Hike 25). Curve to the left 30 yards on the Soldier Pass Trail to the Devil's Kitchen on the right.

After the kitchen, continue heading north up the canyon 100 yards to a junction with the Teacup Trail on the left (Hike 31). Stay to the right, weaving across red dirt and red slab rock through an open forest. Dramatic red rock formations surround the trail. Follow the east wall of the canyon through eroding sedimentary formations to a flat slick rock area on the left at Seven Sacred Pools. After exploring the pools, continue along the trail located behind the pools to the east. Wind through the forest along the contours of the hillside to the posted wilderness boundary by the streambed at the far end of the jeep access road. Pass the boundary gate and walk up the canyon floor to a Y-fork. The left fork continues to Soldier Pass at the head of the canyon on Brins Mesa (Hike 29). Stay to the right, walking straight ahead towards the arches. Ascend the east canyon wall on natural red rock steps to a large slab rock knoll with 360-degree views. Climb the hill to a ledge on the mountain wall. The steep, narrow path scrambles up to two of the arches in a cave-like setting. The third arch is reached on a faint, cliffside path to the left.

Hike 29
Devil's Kitchen •
Seven Sacred Pools • Brins Mesa
SOLDIER PASS TRAIL

Hiking distance: 4.5 miles round trip
Hiking time: 2.5 hours
Elevation gain: 450 feet
Maps: U.S.G.S. Wilson Mountain
      Beartooth Publishing—Sedona, AZ

map
next page

Summary of hike: The Soldier Pass Trail climbs to expansive views from Soldier Pass atop Brins Mesa, an 800-foot table-top plateau above Sedona. The trail ascends Soldier Wash, the draw between the mesa, and the 6,355-foot Capitol Butte. At the mouth of the canyon, near the base of Coffeepot Rock, is a woodland of Arizona cypress. At the head of the canyon, atop the ridge at Brins Mesa, is a forest of pinyon pine and juniper. En route, the trail visits Devil's Kitchen, a cavernous 65-foot-deep sinkhole formed in 1888, and Seven Sacred Pools, a series of descending creek bed pools naturally carved in the slick rock. Throughout the hike, the scenic canyon landscape is punctuated with weather-sculpted columnar formations.

Driving directions: From the Sedona Y (Highways 89A and 179 junction), drive 1.3 miles southwest on Highway 89A (towards Cottonwood) to Soldier Pass Road in West Sedona. Turn right and drive 1.4 miles to Rim Shadows Drive. Turn right and continue 0.2 miles to the Soldier Pass Trailhead parking lot on the left.

Hiking directions: Follow the hiking directions for Hike 28 to the trail junction for the Soldier Pass Arches. The right fork leads to the Soldier Pass Arches (Hike 28). Take the narrower left fork towards Soldier Pass, staying near the canyon bottom. The arches can be seen on the east canyon wall. Climb to a ridge and follow the ridge north, ascending nearly 400 feet. At the top, the path levels out and crosses Soldier Pass. Descend east to a T-junction with the Brins Mesa Trail.

To extend the hike, the left fork leads 2 miles northwest to the parking area on Dry Creek Road (Hike 53). The right fork leads a half mile southeast to the rim above Mormon Canyon (Hike 27).

HIKES 28 • 29
DEVIL'S KITCHEN
SEVEN SACRED POOLS
SOLDIER PASS ARCHES
BRINS MESA
SOLDIER PASS TRAIL

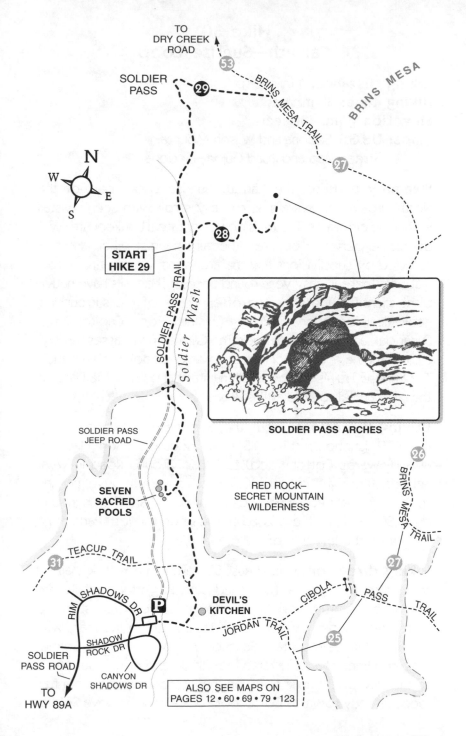

TO
DRY CREEK
ROAD

53

SOLDIER
PASS

29

BRINS MESA TRAIL

BRINS MESA

27

N
W   E
S

28

START
HIKE 29

SOLDIER PASS TRAIL

Soldier Wash

SOLDIER PASS ARCHES

26

SOLDIER PASS
JEEP ROAD

BRINS MESA TRAIL

**SEVEN
SACRED
POOLS**

RED ROCK–
SECRET MOUNTAIN
WILDERNESS

TEACUP TRAIL

31

27

CIBOLA   PASS   TRAIL

RIM SHADOWS DR

P

**DEVIL'S
KITCHEN**

JORDAN TRAIL

25

SHADOW
ROCK DR

SOLDIER
PASS ROAD

CANYON
SHADOWS DR

TO
HWY 89A

ALSO SEE MAPS ON
PAGES 12 • 60 • 69 • 79 • 123

Hike 30
Carruth—Sunrise Loop

Hiking distance: 1 mile loop
Hiking time: 30 minutes
Elevation gain: 100 feet
Maps: U.S.G.S. Sedona and Wilson Mountain
      Street Map and Road Guide—Sedona

Summary of hike: The Carruth—Sunrise Loop, part of the North Urban Trail System, is an easy stroll with scenic vistas within the city limits. The trails do not create a backcountry wilderness experience, but are rather a relaxing stroll on land surrounded by subdivisions and the area's many natural rock formations. There is easy year-round access. The trails have native plant identification signs and offer views of the surrounding geological formations, including Chimney Rock, Capitol Butte, Sugarloaf, and Coffeepot Rock. The Carruth Trail passes through a pinyon pine and juniper forest to an overlook with a bench. The Sunrise Trail is a wide, well maintained path at the base of the hill, parallel to Soldier Pass Road.

Driving directions: From the Sedona Y (Highways 89A and 179 junction), drive 1.5 miles southwest on Highway 89A (towards Cottonwood) to Posse Ground Road in West Sedona. Turn right and drive 0.6 miles to Carruth Drive, curving to the right past Posse Grounds Community Park. Turn right and drive 80 yards to the posted trailhead on the left. Park in the pullout on the left side of the road.

Hiking directions: Head east 50 yards to a Y-fork, parallel to Carruth Drive on the rock-lined path. Begin the loop to the left on the Carruth Trail. Stroll through an open forest mixed with pinyon pines, Arizona cypress, and shrub live oak, with views of Munds Mountain, Schnebly Hill, Mitten Ridge, Soldier Pass, and Brins Mesa. Traverse the hillside and climb rock steps to the hilltop. Continue north on the interpretive trail to a trail loop, directly towards Coffeepot Rock and high above Soldier

Pass Road. Take the left fork on the small loop, walking clock-wise. Just before completing the loop, bear left on the Sunrise Trail. Meander downhill along the wide, forested path. Head south, parallel to Soldier Pass Road, and return to Carruth Drive. Curve right, staying on the trail running parallel to Carruth Drive, and wind easily uphill back to the trailhead.

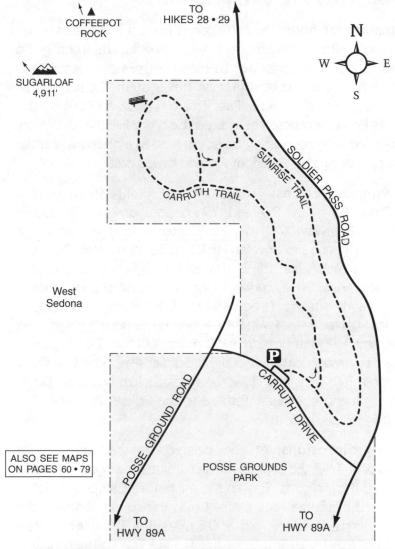

COFFEEPOT
ROCK

TO
HIKES 28 • 29

N
W E
S

SUGARLOAF
4,911'

SOLDIER PASS ROAD

SUNRISE TRAIL

CARRUTH TRAIL

West
Sedona

P

CARRUTH DRIVE

POSSE GROUND ROAD

ALSO SEE MAPS
ON PAGES 60 • 79

POSSE GROUNDS
PARK

TO
HWY 89A

TO
HWY 89A

CARRUTH–SUNRISE LOOP

Hike 31
Teacup Trail

Hiking distance: 3.2 miles round trip
Hiking time: 1.5 hour
Elevation gain: 150 feet
Maps: U.S.G.S. Sedona and Wilson Mountain

map next page

Summary of hike: The caffeinated Teacup Trail passes under Coffeepot Rock along the massive red rock cliffs fronting the north edge of Sedona. The 1.8-mile trail links the eastern and western trails of the North Urban Trail System. The scenic trail connects with the Soldier Pass Trail (Hikes 28 and 29) by the Devil's Kitchen sinkhole. The trail can be hiked in either direction, extended with connecting trails, or hiked as a one-way shuttle. This hike begins by Sugarloaf Hill and heads east.

Driving directions: TO SUGARLOAF TRAILHEAD: From the Sedona Y (Highways 89A and 179 junction), drive 2 miles southwest on Highway 89A (towards Cottonwood) to Coffee Pot Road. Turn right and drive 0.6 miles to Sanborn Drive. Turn left and go 2 blocks to Little Elf Drive. Turn right and go 2 blocks to Buena Vista Drive, curving right. The trailhead parking lot is immediately on the left, across from 2045 Buena Vista Drive.

TO SOLDIER PASS TRAILHEAD: From the Sedona Y (Highways 89A and 179 junction), drive 1.3 miles southwest on Highway 89A (towards Cottonwood) to Soldier Pass Road in West Sedona. Turn right and drive 1.4 miles to Rim Shadows Drive. Turn right and continue 0.2 miles to the Soldier Pass Trailhead parking lot on the left.

Hiking directions: At the posted trailhead are several trail forks. Take the signed Teacup Trail to the right, and head toward the red cliffs. Stay to the right at another posted junction, and climb the rock steps. Cross the rolling foothills to a T-junction under utility lines at 0.3 miles. The Thunder Mountain Trail (Hike 34) goes left. Take the Teacup Trail to the right 100 yards to another junction. The Sugarloaf Summit Loop (Hike

33) goes to the right. Continue straight on the Teacup Trail 250 yards to an unsigned Y-fork, marked with stones. The left fork leads to the base of Coffeepot Rock (Hike 32). Stay to the right 0.1 miles to a posted junction. Bear left and descend into the draw to the base of the enormous red cliff wall beneath Coffeepot Rock, located on the southeast tip of the massive cliffs. The undulating path meanders past large boulders in a forest of Arizona cypress. Follow the contours of the hillside perched on rock slabs and red dirt, overlooking Sedona. Drop down to the Soldier Pass Jeep Road, and follow the road 20 yards to the right. Bear left on the signed trail, and climb to a junction with the Soldier Pass Trail (Hike 29) where the Teacup Trail ends. A hundred yards to the right is the Devil's Kitchen sinkhole. Return along the same route.

Hike 32
Coffeepot Rock

Hiking distance: 1 mile round trip
Hiking time: 45 minutes
Elevation gain: 400 feet
Maps: U.S.G.S. Sedona and Wilson Mountain

map
next page

Summary of hike: The prominent Coffeepot Rock is shaped like a percolator style coffee pot with a spout. The richly colored formation is visible from the entire Sedona area, lying amongst the massive cliffs fronting the town's north edge. It forms the west wall of the entrance to Soldier Wash. This hike begins on the Teacup Trail and leads up to a rock ledge under the spout of Coffeepot Rock.

Driving directions: From the Sedona Y (Highways 89A and 179 junction), drive 2 miles southwest on Highway 89A (towards Cottonwood) to Coffee Pot Road. Turn right and drive 0.6 miles to Sanborn Drive. Turn left and go 2 blocks to Little Elf Drive. Turn right and go 2 blocks to Buena Vista Drive, curving right. The Sugarloaf Trailhead parking lot is immediately on the left, across from 2045 Buena Vista Drive.

Hiking directions: At the posted trailhead are several trail forks. Take the signed Teacup Trail to the right, and head toward the red cliffs. Stay to the right at another posted junction, and climb the rock steps. Cross the rolling foothills to a T-junction under utility lines at 0.3 miles. The Thunder Mountain Trail (Hike 34) goes left. Take the Teacup Trail to the right 100 yards to another junction. The Sugarloaf Summit Loop (Hike 33) goes to the right. Continue straight on the Teacup Trail 250 yards to an unsigned Y-fork, marked with stones. The Teacup Trail (Hike 31) continues to the right. Take the left fork, leaving the main trail, and head uphill to an overlook of the red rock formations. Continue towards prominent Coffeepot Rock at the base of the cliffs. Curve right on a rock slab, and follow the rock shelf along the base of the sculpted formations high above West Sedona. As you near the coffee spout and the trail fades, you can explore the various levels and details of the rock. Return by retracing your steps.

COFFEEPOT ROCK

HIKE 31

TEACUP TRAIL

HIKE 32

COFFEEPOT ROCK

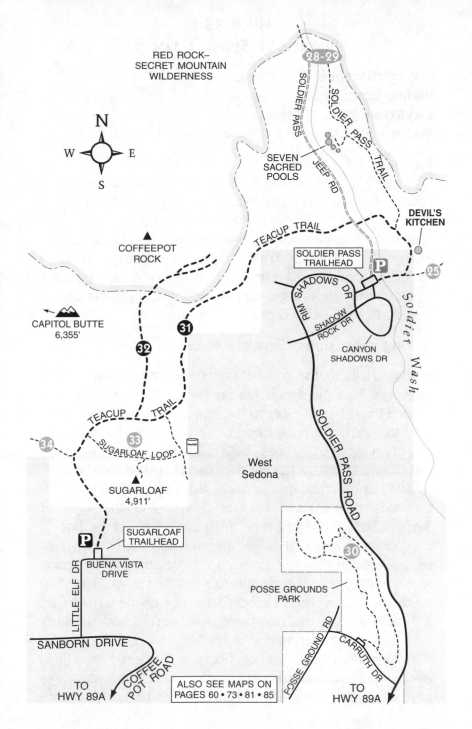

RED ROCK–
SECRET MOUNTAIN
WILDERNESS

28-29

SOLDIER PASS

SOLDIER PASS TRAIL

N
W E
S

SEVEN
SACRED
POOLS

JEEP RD

DEVIL'S
KITCHEN

TEACUP TRAIL

COFFEEPOT
ROCK

SOLDIER PASS
TRAILHEAD

P

25

CAPITOL BUTTE
6,355'

RIM SHADOWS DR

SHADOW
ROCK DR

Soldier Wash

31

32

CANYON
SHADOWS DR

TEACUP TRAIL

34

33

SUGARLOAF LOOP

WATER

West
Sedona

SOLDIER PASS ROAD

SUGARLOAF
4,911'

P

SUGARLOAF
TRAILHEAD

30

LITTLE ELF DR

BUENA VISTA
DRIVE

POSSE GROUNDS
PARK

SANBORN DRIVE

COFFEE POT ROAD

FOSSE GROUND RD

CARRUTH DR

TO
HWY 89A

ALSO SEE MAPS ON
PAGES 60 • 73 • 81 • 85

TO
HWY 89A

Hike 33
Sugarloaf Summit Loop

Hiking distance: 2 mile loop
Hiking time: 1 hour
Elevation gain: 400 feet
Maps: U.S.G.S. Sedona and Wilson Mountain

Summary of hike: Located on the north edge of Sedona, Sugarloaf Hill is a rounded 250-foot butte overlooking West Sedona. The bald, red rock mound is due south of Coffeepot Rock and east of Chimney Rock. From below, it does not appear that the views atop Sugarloaf Hill would be spectacular. From the 4,911-foot summit, they are awesome, with close-up 360-degree vistas. It is an easy climb to the summit from the tapered north slope. Sugarloaf Hill is accessed from the Teacup Trail, part of the North Urban Trail System.

Driving directions: Same as Hike 32.

Hiking directions: At the posted trailhead are several trail forks. Take the signed Teacup Trail to the right, and head toward the red cliffs. Stay to the right at another posted junction, and climb the rock steps. Cross the rolling foothills to a T-junction under utility lines at 0.3 miles. The Thunder Mountain Trail (Hike 34) goes left. Take the Teacup Trail to the right 100 yards to another posted junction. The Teacup Trail (Hike 31) continues straight ahead. Take the right fork on the Sugarloaf Summit Loop, leaving the main trail. Head south up the sloping backside of Sugarloaf Hill. The cairn-marked path curves east and traverses the hillside, parallel to utility poles, to a junction at the northeast corner of the rounded formation. The loop continues straight ahead. Detour to the right on the Summit Trail, and climb a short distance to the exposed, rounded hilltop. After studying the landscape and picking out landmarks, return to the Sugarloaf Loop junction. Continue to the right and head east. Gradually curve left to a T-junction just before reaching a large water tank. Take the left fork 0.2 miles to a posted junction with the Teacup Trail. The right fork descends along the base of Coffeepot Rock to the Soldier Pass Trail (Hike 31). Take the left fork and return to the west, passing the Coffeepot Trail on the right and completing the loop.

COFFEEPOT ROCK

TO
SOLDIER PASS
TRAIL

CAPITOL BUTTE
6,355'

THUNDER MOUNTAIN TRAIL

TO
CHIMNEY
ROCK

TEACUP TRAIL

SUGARLOAF LOOP

WATER

SUGARLOAF
4,911'

N
W — E
S

P
SUGARLOAF
TRAILHEAD

BUENA VISTA
DRIVE

LITTLE ELF DR

West
Sedona

ALSO SEE MAPS
ON PAGES 60 • 79 • 85

SANBORN DRIVE

SUGARLOAF SUMMIT

Hike 34
Thunder Mountain Trail

Hiking distance: 4 miles round trip
Hiking time: 2 hours
Elevation gain: 50 feet
Maps: U.S.G.S. Sedona and Wilson Mountain

map
next page

Summary of hike: The Thunder Mountain Trail follows the southern base of Chimney Rock and the sheer south face of Capitol Butte along the north edge of Sedona. Capitol Butte (also known as Thunder Mountain) extends to a height of 6,355 feet, making it the highest rock formation in Sedona. The Thunder Mountain Trail is a connector trail between the eastern and western trails of the North Urban Trail System. This hike begins from the west end by Chimney Rock and heads east to the Teacup Trail (Hike 31) and Sugarloaf Hill (Hike 33) near the Sugarloaf Trailhead. The trail can be hiked in either direction, extended with connecting trails, or hiked as a one-way shuttle.

Driving directions: TO THUNDER MOUNTAIN TRAILHEAD: From the Sedona Y (Highways 89A and 179 junction), drive 3.1 miles southwest on Highway 89A (towards Cottonwood) to Dry Creek Road. Turn right and drive 0.5 miles to Thunder Mountain Road. Turn right and drive 0.5 miles to the posted trailhead parking lot on the left. Turn left and go 0.1 miles to the parking lot.

TO SUGARLOAF TRAILHEAD: From the Sedona Y (Highways 89A and 179 junction), drive 2 miles southwest on Highway 89A (towards Cottonwood) to Coffee Pot Road. Turn right and drive 0.6 miles to Sanborn Drive. Turn left and go 2 blocks to Little Elf Drive. Turn right and go 2 blocks to Buena Vista Drive, curving right. The trailhead parking lot is immediately on the left, across from 2045 Buena Vista Drive.

Hiking directions: Take the posted Thunder Mountain Trail north under power lines to the Chimney Rock–Thunder Mountain Trail junction. The left fork leads to Chimney Rock

(Hikes 35—37). Follow the Thunder Mountain Trail to the right, skirting the south edge of Chimney Rock. The path roughly follows the power poles through a mixed forest of junipers and pines to a junction with the Chimney Pass Trail on the left. Continue straight ahead on the undulating path along the base of Capitol Butte. Cross a forested draw and the open scrub-covered terrain, with great views of the weather-carved red rock. Walk across a slick rock drainage to a posted junction at 2 miles, where the Thunder Mountain Trail ends.

The right fork leads to the Sugarloaf Trailhead on Buena Vista Drive. The Teacup Trail continues straight ahead to the Soldier Pass Trail (Hikes 28 and 29), en route passing Coffeepot Rock (Hike 32) and Sugarloaf Hill (Hike 33). Return by retracing your steps.

Hike 35
Chimney Rock Loop

Hiking distance: 2.3 mile loop
Hiking time: 1 hour
Elevation gain: 300 feet
Maps: U.S.G.S. Sedona and Wilson Mountain

map
next page

Summary of hike: Chimney Rock is a prominent Sedona landmark forming the natural division between West Sedona and the Dry Creek Basin. The Chimney Rock Loop begins just south of Chimney Rock and Capitol Butte at the west end of the North Urban Trail System. The trail circles Chimney Rock, crossing over a narrow pass separating it from Capitol Butte. Throughout the hike are vistas of Cockscomb, Doe Mountain, Lizard Head, Sugarloaf, and Coffeepot Rock.

Driving directions: From the Sedona Y (Highways 89A and 179 junction), drive 3.1 miles southwest on Highway 89A (towards Cottonwood) to Dry Creek Road. Turn right and drive 0.5 miles to Thunder Mountain Road. Turn right and drive 0.5 miles to the posted trailhead parking lot on the left. Turn left and go 0.1 miles to the parking lot.

Hiking directions: Take the posted Thunder Mountain Trail north toward the red rock buttes to the Chimney Rock–Thunder Mountain Trail junction. The right fork follows the southern base of Chimney Rock and the 6,355-foot Capitol Butte (Hike 34). Begin the loop to the left on the Chimney Rock Trail. Continue 300 yards to a saddle and a junction between Chimney Rock on the right and Lower Chimney Rock (also referred to as Chimney Hill) on the left. The left fork leads to the summit of Lower Chimney Rock and also loops around the lower slopes (Hikes 36 and 37). Take the north fork to the right toward the base of Chimney Rock. Follow the cairn-marked trail up the west side of Chimney Rock to vistas across the Dry Creek Basin, including Lizard Rock (extending off the west summit of Capitol Butte), Cockscomb, and Doe Mountain. Curve east through

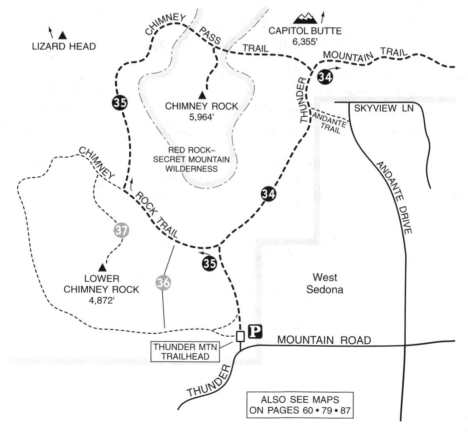

the forested canyon between Capitol Butte, with its sculpted spires, and Chimney Rock, offering a unique north view of the chimney's stack. An unmarked but distinct side path on the right climbs past small arches and caves to the base of the chimney stack. Return to the main trail, and climb out of the canyon along the base of Chimney Rock, emerging at an overlook of West Sedona, Munds Mountain, Mitten Ridge, Sugarloaf, and Snoopy Rock. Descend along the east side of Chimney Rock, where there is a distinctly different view of the chimney. Traverse the cliffside path to a junction with the Thunder Mountain Trail. Go to the right and follow the south edge of Chimney Rock past the Andante Trail, a connector trail on the left. Complete the loop and return to the left.

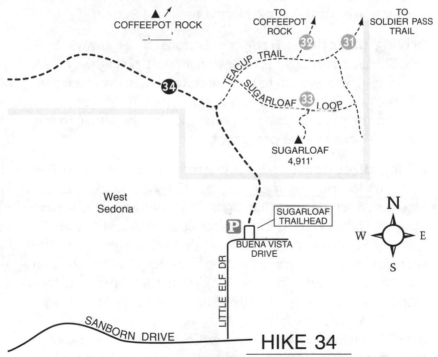

HIKE 34
THUNDER MOUNTAIN
HIKE 35
CHIMNEY ROCK

Hike 36
Lower Chimney Rock Loop
(CHIMNEY HILL)

Hiking distance: 1.5 mile loop
Hiking time: 45 minutes
Elevation gain: 100 feet
Maps: U.S.G.S. Sedona and Wilson Mountain

Summary of hike: The Lower Chimney Rock Trail follows the western slope of Chimney Rock, circling Lower Chimney Rock along the east edge of the Dry Creek Basin. The path meanders through a juniper forest with views of Capitol Butte, Lizard Head, and Cockscomb. The Lower Chimney Rock Trail is the westernmost trail in the North Urban Trail System.

Driving directions: From the Sedona Y (Highways 89A and 179 junction), drive 3.1 miles southwest on Highway 89A (towards Cottonwood) to Dry Creek Road. Turn right and drive 0.5 miles to Thunder Mountain Road. Turn right and drive 0.5 miles to the posted trailhead parking lot on the left. Turn left and go 0.1 miles to the parking lot.

Hiking directions: Take the posted Thunder Mountain Trail north under power lines to the Chimney Rock–Thunder Mountain Trail junction. The right fork follows the southern base of Chimney Rock and Capitol Butte (Hike 34). Take the Chimney Rock Trail on the red dirt path to the left. Continue 0.2 miles to a saddle and a junction between Chimney Rock on the right and Lower Chimney Rock on the left. The right fork loops around Chimney Rock (Hike 35). Stay to the left, straight ahead 20 yards, to another signed junction. The left fork (Hike 37) climbs to the summit of Lower Chimney Rock (also known as Chimney Hill). Continue straight ahead and descend through a forest of junipers, with close-up views of Chimney Rock and Capitol Butte. The expansive vistas extend across the Dry Creek Basin. The winding path meanders downhill to the north and west to a fenceline. Curve left, looping back towards Lower

Chimney Rock. Follow the cairn-marked path around the west side of the rounded 4,872-foot hill. Pass through a trail gate, and continue on the south edge of the sculpted hill. Parallel the utility poles to a trail split. Veer to the right 30 yards, returning to the southwest corner of the trailhead parking lot.

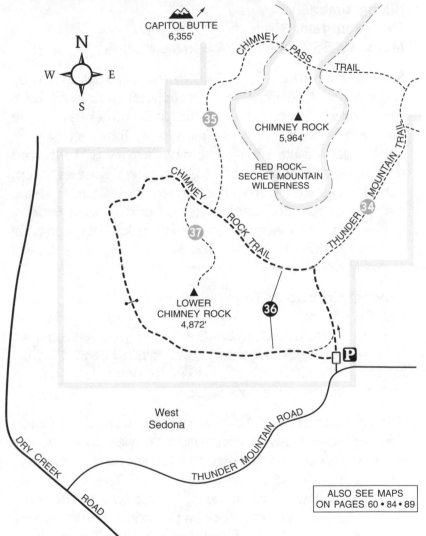

LOWER CHIMNEY ROCK
(CHIMNEY HILL)

Hike 37
Lower Chimney Rock Trail to the
Chimney Hill Summit

Hiking distance: 0.8 miles round trip
Hiking time: 30 minutes
Elevation gain: 350 feet
Maps: U.S.G.S. Sedona and Wilson Mountain

Summary of hike: Lower Chimney Rock (also called Chimney Hill) is a bald 4,872-foot hill just southwest of Chimney Rock. The rounded hill is on the east edge of Dry Creek Basin at the west end of the North Urban Trail System. This hike begins on the Thunder Mountain Trail and climbs Chimney Hill to the red rock summit. From the trailhead, the ascent appears steep, but it is an easy climb from the tapered north slope. From the summit are great 360-degree vistas, including West Sedona, Cockscomb, Doe Mountain, Cottonwood, Bell Rock, Cathedral Rock, Courthouse Butte, Table Top Mountain, Schnebly Hill, and Munds Mountain.

Driving directions: From the Sedona Y (Highways 89A and 179 junction), drive 3.1 miles southwest on Highway 89A (towards Cottonwood) to Dry Creek Road. Turn right and drive 0.5 miles to Thunder Mountain Road. Turn right and drive 0.5 miles to the posted trailhead parking lot on the left. Turn left and go 0.1 miles to the parking lot.

Hiking directions: Take the posted Thunder Mountain Trail north under power lines to the Chimney Rock–Thunder Mountain Trail junction. The right fork follows the southern base of Chimney Rock and Capitol Butte (Hike 34). Take the Chimney Rock Trail to the left. Continue 300 yards to a saddle and a junction between Chimney Rock on the right and Little Chimney Rock on the left. The right fork loops around Chimney Rock (Hike 35). Stay to the left, straight ahead 20 yards, to another signed junction. The right fork, again straight ahead, loops around the lower forested slope (Hike 36). Bear left and head up the mountain to the south, steadily climbing to great vistas. On the upper portion of the climb, the trail winds up the east face and curves back for a final ascent. Atop the bald red rock summit, cross the rounded slope and descend to the southern tip, overlooking West Sedona with sweeping 360-degree panoramas.

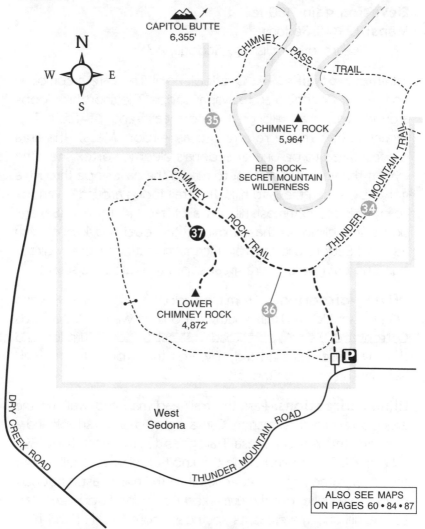

ALSO SEE MAPS
ON PAGES 60 • 84 • 87

LOWER CHIMNEY ROCK
TO CHIMNEY HILL SUMMIT

Hike 38
Overlook Point Trails
TABLE TOP MOUNTAIN

Hiking distance: 0.5 mile loop
Hiking time: 30 minutes
Elevation gain: 100 feet
Maps: U.S.G.S. Sedona
      Beartooth Publishing—Sedona, AZ

Summary of hike: The Overlook Point Trails are a combination of the Coconino and Yavapai Loops. The short hike loops around two small hills on the northeast end of Table Top Mountain (commonly referred to as Airport Mesa). This area is considered to be one of Sedona's electric vortex sites. The eye of the vortex is thought to run up the east slope through a gorge between the two hills. The trail loops around Overlook Point, the southernmost hill, on a cliff-edge terrace. Several side paths climb to the summit of the bald red knobs, with vistas of Sedona and the magnificent formations in every direction. The twin summits are great spots to watch the sunset.

Driving directions: From the Sedona Y (Highways 89A and 179 junction), drive 1 mile southwest on Highway 89A (towards Cottonwood) to Airport Road in West Sedona. Turn left and drive 0.5 miles up the road, towards the airport, to the trailhead parking area on the left.

Hiking directions: Pass the trailhead map and walk up the eroded red rock formation. Curve right to an overlook and a junction. The Airport Mesa Trail goes to the right (Hike 39). Take the left path and circle the knoll clockwise, well below the summit. The large rounded knoll to the northeast is not part of this loop hike, but the unmarked Coconino Loop veers left to the hill and traverses its southeast contours. For this hike, stay to the right. Several unmarked paths climb up the formation to Overlook Point, the bald, rounded summit with a lone, windswept pine. Numerous routes curve around the knoll and up to the 4,692-foot summit, for great vistas and soaking in energy. To extend the hike, the Airport Mesa Trail circles Table Top Mountain (Hike 39).

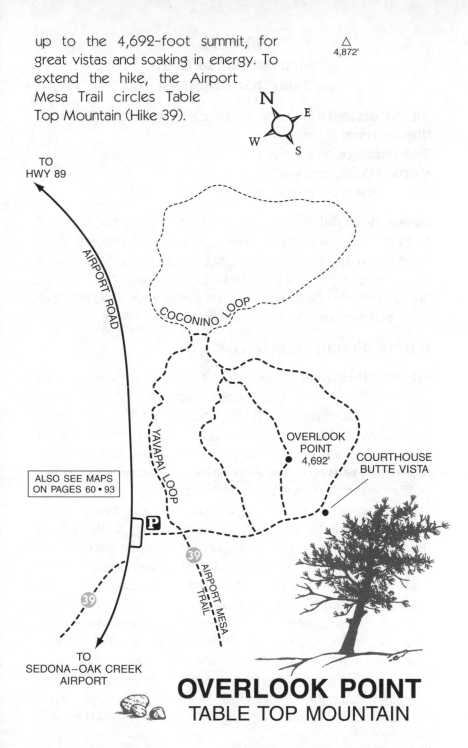

△
4,872'

TO
HWY 89

AIRPORT ROAD

COCONINO LOOP

YAVAPAI LOOP

ALSO SEE MAPS
ON PAGES 60 • 93

OVERLOOK
POINT
4,692'

COURTHOUSE
BUTTE VISTA

P

39

39

AIRPORT MESA
TRAIL

TO
SEDONA–OAK CREEK
AIRPORT

OVERLOOK POINT
TABLE TOP MOUNTAIN

Hike 39
Airport Mesa Trail
TABLE TOP MOUNTAIN

Hiking distance: 4.3 mile loop (including the Table Top Trail)
Hiking time: 2 hours
Elevation gain: 200 feet
Maps: U.S.G.S. Sedona
       Beartooth Publishing—Sedona, AZ

Summary of hike: The Airport Mesa Trail, in the heart of Sedona, circles the upper slopes of Table Top Mountain on the edge of a 4,600-foot terrace. It is a great hike for studying the geography of the entire Sedona area, viewing the endless display of red rock formations, and experiencing the energies of one of Sedona's well-known vortex sites.

Driving directions: Same as Hike 38.

Hiking directions: Walk past the Overlook Point trailhead map, and curve right to the saddle and signed Airport Loop Trail. Head south, perched on the red rock hillside, with views across lower Oak Creek Valley, Bell Rock, and the Village of Oak Creek. Curve to the south face of Table Top Mountain (commonly referred to as Airport Mesa). Follow the contours of the hillside over basalt boulders and through groves of pin-yon pine, cypress, juniper, scrub oak, and a variety of cactus. At the southwest corner of the mountain, parallel the airport fence at the end of the runway. Curve left to a posted junction with the Table Top Trail on the left at 1.7 miles. Detour left on this trail, and descend along the ridge to a saddle. Climb the sloping ridge south on the long, narrow finger of land. The path loops around the point, with two cypress trees gracing the tip at a half mile. Return to the Airport Loop Trail, and continue to a bird's-eye view of West Sedona. The path then steadily slopes downhill and zigzags down two switchbacks. At the second switchback is a junction. The Bandit Trail winds down the hillside to the left, connecting with the Ridge Trail (Hike 41).

Just past the Bandit Trail, an unmarked but distinct path veers left down the hillside to the corner of Sunset Drive and Shelby Drive. Continue traversing the north-facing slope, returning to Airport Road across from the trailhead.

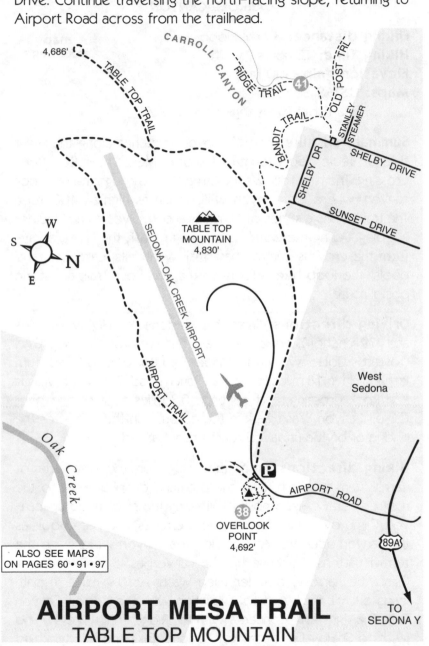

AIRPORT MESA TRAIL
TABLE TOP MOUNTAIN

Hike 40
Carroll Canyon Wash—Old Post Loop
CARROLL CANYON

Hiking distance: 3.3 mile loop
Hiking time: 1.5 hours
Elevation gain: 300 feet
Maps: U.S.G.S. Sedona
       Beartooth Publishing—Sedona, AZ

*map
next page*

Summary of hike: Carroll Canyon stretches along the west side of Table Top Mountain (Airport Mesa) near Red Rock Crossing. The hike follows the streambed through the red rock canyon, where the canyon walls reach as high as 400 feet. The trail climbs a series of terraces and involves some boulder hopping. During the winter and spring runoff, the quiet, away-from-the-crowds canyon has small waterfalls, cascades, and pools. The loop hike returns on the Old Post Trail, a historic postal route.

Driving directions: From the Sedona Y (Highways 89A and 179 junction), drive 4.2 miles southwest on Highway 89A (towards Cottonwood) to Upper Red Rock Loop Road. Turn left and drive 1.8 miles to Chavez Ranch Road. Turn left towards Red Rock Crossing, and continue 0.3 miles to a bridge over Carroll Canyon Wash. Park in the pullouts on the left after the bridge or on the unpaved road straight ahead.

Hiking directions: From the bridge on the east side of Carroll Canyon Wash, take the path and drop down into the red rock draw. Head north, following the streambed up canyon. Climb over the water-carved terraces, and pass pools as the canyon deepens. At 1.2 miles, the canyon widens and the terrain flattens. Continue up the canyon as it narrows again. Climb the narrow, boulder-filled wash. At 0.9 miles, a path leads out of the wash to a junction with the Carroll Canyon Trail. The right fork connects with the Ridge Trail (Hike 41) and leads to Shelby Drive in West Sedona. Take the left fork and head west, traversing the canyon wall. Cross over a ridge to a junction with the Old Post Trail. Bear left on the old mail route and descend, passing the Herkenham Trail on the right. Continue straight ahead, returning to Chavez Road 0.15 miles west of the trailhead. Head down the road to the left to complete the loop.

Hike 41
Old Post—Carroll Canyon—
Ridge Trails Loop
CARROLL CANYON

Hiking distance: 3.4 mile loop
Hiking time: 1.5 hours
Elevation gain: 200 feet
Maps: U.S.G.S. Sedona
       Beartooth Publishing—Sedona, AZ

map
next page

Summary of hike: The Carroll Canyon Area Trails are a network of trails that crisscross the low hills between Table Top Mountain (Airport Mesa) and Scheurman Mountain. The trails weave through the red rock landscape, crossing rolling hills in a pristine pinyon and juniper woodland. Small canyons, rocky gorges, streambeds, and seasonal streams are scattered throughout the area. Five trailheads access the Carroll Canyon trails, offering various loop hikes and one-way shuttles. This hike begins on the Old Post Trail, a historic postal route, and forms a loop through the scenic hills.

Driving directions: From the Sedona Y (Highways 89A and 179 junction), drive 2.2 miles southwest on Highway 89A (towards Cottonwood) to Shelby Drive. Turn left and drive 0.6 miles to La Entrada office building parking lot on the right at 2155 Shelby Drive, 10 yards past Stanley Steamer Drive. Turn right into the parking lot to the 3 designated trailhead parking spaces at the back end of the parking lot.

Hiking directions: Pass the trailhead map to a posted junction with the Ridge Trail. Begin the loop to the right on the Old

Post Trail. Cross the rolling terrain west, away from Table Top Mountain, through groves of Arizona cypress and junipers. Follow the north boundary of the open space, and descend towards a residential area to a posted junction. Bear left, staying on the Old Post Trail. Pass a junction with the Carroll Canyon Trail on the left, and cross a wash to a great view of Cathedral Rock. The red dirt path steadily dips and rises through the rolling hills. Head up a draw to the west flank of a hill. Descend the slope and drop into a canyon to a signed junction on the canyon floor. Leave the Old Post Trail, and bear left on the Carroll Canyon Trail. Snake up the canyon wall and cross a ridge. Drop down into Carroll Canyon beneath Table Top Mountain. Traverse the west canyon wall in a small side canyon. Loop across the side canyon, and double back on the east wall, returning to the main canyon. Cross the wash to a junction with the Ridge Trail coming in from the right. Continue straight, as the two trails join for a few hundred yards, to a trail split. The Carroll Canyon Trail goes left. Stay straight on the Ridge Trail, weaving north. Cross a series of slick rock washes, and pass the Bandit Trail on the right. Return to the trailhead 50 yards ahead.

HIKE 40
CARROLL CANYON– OLD POST LOOP
HIKE 41
OLD POST–CARROLL CANYON– RIDGE TRAIL LOOP

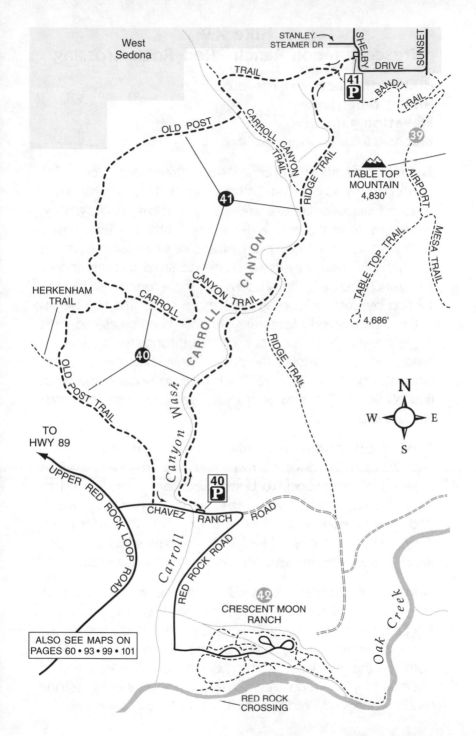

West
Sedona

STANLEY
STEAMER DR

SHELBY

DRIVE

SUNSET

TRAIL

BANDIT

TRAIL

41
P

OLD POST

CARROLL CANYON TRAIL

RIDGE TRAIL

39

TABLE TOP
MOUNTAIN
4,830'

AIRPORT

MESA TRAIL

TABLE TOP TRAIL

41

CARROLL

CANYON

CANYON TRAIL

4,686'

HERKENHAM
TRAIL

CARROLL

RIDGE TRAIL

OLD POST TRAIL

40

Canyon Wash

N
W   E
S

TO
HWY 89

UPPER RED ROCK LOOP ROAD

40
P

CHAVEZ

RANCH

ROAD

Carroll

RED ROCK ROAD

42
CRESCENT MOON
RANCH

Oak Creek

ALSO SEE MAPS ON
PAGES 60 • 93 • 99 • 101

RED ROCK
CROSSING

Hike 42
Crescent Moon Ranch—Red Rock Crossing

Hiking distance: 1.5 miles round trip
Hiking time: 1 hour
Elevation gain: Level
Maps: U.S.G.S. Sedona

Summary of hike: Crescent Moon Ranch lies along Oak Creek directly across from Cathedral Rock. The ranch is a beautiful and popular day-use area for picnicking, photography, wading, sunbathing, and walking. The Cathedral Rock vistas seen in so many photographs of the area were taken from this location. This hike is a scenic creekside stroll through riparian vegetation beneath the shadow of the eroding red buttes, framed by cottonwood and sycamore trees. The trail begins in the meadow and passes the old John Lee homestead, built in the late 1800s. (The section of trail through the meadow is handicapped accessible.) The path follows the creek upstream along the base of Cathedral Rock to a vortex site known as Buddah Beach. The area is studded with hundreds of hand-stacked prayer rocks.

Driving directions: From the Sedona Y (Highways 89A and 179 junction), drive 4.2 miles southwest on Highway 89A (towards Cottonwood) to Upper Red Rock Loop Road. Turn left and drive 1.8 miles to Chavez Ranch Road. Turn left towards Red Rock Crossing, and continue 0.4 miles to Red Rock Road. Curve right to the posted Red Rock Crossing—Crescent Moon Ranch entrance on the left. An entrance fee is required.

Hiking directions: Fifty yards from the entrance station, take the paved pink path to the north bank of Oak Creek beneath the shadow of gorgeous Cathedral Rock. Follow the creek upstream on the edge of the grassy meadow. Spur paths on the right lead to sitting benches. At the east end of the meadow is the John Lee homestead cabin, a mill, a historic water wheel, and a red rock building, once part of the old OK

Ranch and Chavez Ranch. Leave the paved path and follow the dirt path east along Oak Creek. Stroll through the forest and lush vegetation beneath the north base of Cathedral Rock. Follow a creek channel to a red rock shelf, and rejoin the main channel at a left bend in the creek. Meander through a field of river rocks, across the river from the vertical red rock wall. Walk among the prayer rocks in a clearing at Buddah Beach. The trail soon fades and becomes obscure. Return along the same route.

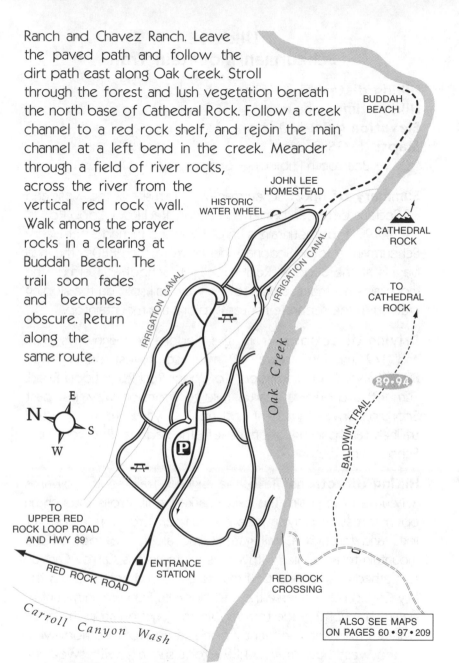

ALSO SEE MAPS
ON PAGES 60 • 97 • 209

CRESCENT MOON RANCH
RED ROCK CROSSING

Hike 43
Scheurman Mountain Trail

Hiking distance: 4.2 miles round trip
Hiking time: 2 hours
Elevation gain: 550 feet
Maps: U.S.G.S. Sedona
      Beartooth Publishing—Sedona, AZ

Summary of hike: Scheurman Mountain sits at the west end of Sedona between Upper and Lower Red Rock Loop Roads. The 4,899-foot mountain is an old volcano named after Henry Scheurman, a local Sedona rancher from the 1880s. The trail begins at the Sedona–Red Rock High School and climbs the mountain's northeast slope to a 3-way trail split on the sloping plateau. Three separate routes explore the mountaintop.

Driving directions: From the Sedona Y (Highways 89A and 179 junction), drive 4.2 miles southwest on Highway 89A (towards Cottonwood) to Upper Red Rock Loop Road. Turn left and drive a quarter mile to Scorpion Way, just past Scorpion Drive. Turn right and go 100 yards to the posted trailhead and parking lot on the left. The Sedona–Red Rock High School is on the right.

Hiking directions: Take the signed trail south towards Scheurman Mountain. The cairn-marked trail strolls through an open forest of pinyon pine and juniper. Cross under power lines and through a trail gate. Climb along the foot of the mountain to a saddle, with views south across Carroll Canyon to Cathedral Rock and Courthouse Butte and north across the Dry Creek area. Traverse the east slope of Scheurman Mountain on an easy uphill grade to a saddle and junction atop the open plateau. The right fork gently climbs a quarter mile northwest to the west side of the 4,899-foot summit, with sweeping vistas in all directions. Return to the junction and continue 50 yards to another trail fork. Take the left fork and head south up the slope, crossing over the rise to the narrow south tip of the mesa, with a fine view across the Oak Creek Valley to Red Rock State Park and House Mountain. Return to the junction and take the remaining fork southwest. Follow the draw downhill to Scheurman Mountain Tank, a manmade cattle pond. Continue descending to the edge of the mesa and an overlook of Red Rock State Park and Oak Creek winding through the deep canyon below. This is our turn-around spot.

To hike farther, the trail drops one mile down the west side of the mountain to Lower Red Rock Loop Road, near the trailhead for the Red Hills (Hike 44). Return along the same route.

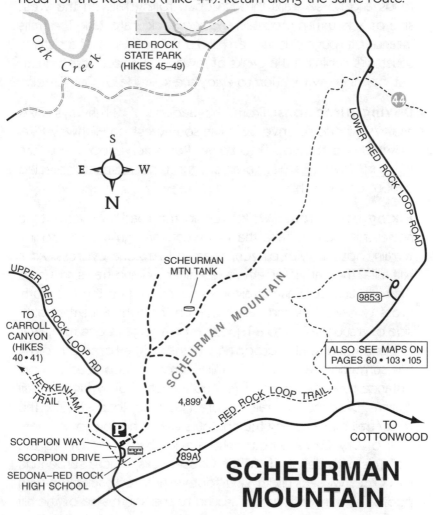

Hike 44
Red Hills to Oak Creek

Hiking distance: 5 miles round trip
Hiking time: 2.5 hours
Elevation gain: 500 feet
Maps: U.S.G.S. Sedona
       Beartooth Publishing—Sedona, AZ

Summary of hike: This hike follows a network of old jeep roads and horse trails through open rolling hills on the west side of Scheurman Mountain and Red Rock State Park. The trails meander through pristine red hills to the remnants of a historic squatter's cabin on the banks of lower Oak Creek. It is a quiet, out-of-the-way location to enjoy the solitude of Oak Creek.

Driving directions: From the Sedona Y (Highways 89A and 179 junction), drive 5.5 miles southwest on Highway 89A (towards Cottonwood) to Lower Red Rock Loop Road. Turn left and drive 1.8 miles to an unsigned, but distinct, graveled turnout on the right.

Hiking directions: Walk back up the road 150 yards to a horse trail marker. Take the trail west through the red rolling terrain, dotted with pinyon pines and Arizona cypress. At a half mile, the path intersects a red dirt road and trail sign. Cross the road and continue straight ahead, staying on the footpath. Cross two washes and pass Trail R on the right. Skirt the south side of a subdivision to a T-junction on a ridge at one mile. Bear left and head south, dropping off the ridge. Forested rolling hills surround the trail. At 1.3 miles, cross a jeep road a short distance to a second road. Pick up the trail, following the Trail A signs. Descend on Trail A (Forest Service Road 9845L). The road/trail curves along the contours of the hillside to an over-look of Dry Creek on the right; a side road veers off to the left. This path descends to the Goosenecks, where serpentine Oak Creek weaves under 200-foot vertical red rock cliffs with pools. The main trail curves around to the south side of the hill to a view of Cathedral Rock and a trail split on a knoll at 2 miles. The left fork is a terraced path, descending on natural rock steps. The right fork is an unpaved road. Both paths rejoin at the bottom of the hill. On the canyon floor, continue south, parallel to Oak Creek. Follow the old ranch road to the grassy meadow at the creek. The road divides at the rock ruins of an old cabin. The left fork leads 50 yards to the banks of the creek. The main road follows Oak Creek downstream and ends in less than a quarter mile. Explore the area and return along the same route.

ROCK CABIN RUINS

Oak Creek

THE GOOSENECKS

KNOLL

Dry Creek

4,100'

TRAIL A

TO RED ROCK STATE PARK

DRY CREEK OVERLOOK

OLD WAGON ROAD

9845L

P

LOWER RED ROCK LOOP ROAD

SUBDIVISION

TRAIL R

TO SCHEURMAN MOUNTAIN (HIKE 43)

S

E — W

N

SCHEURMAN MOUNTAIN 4,899'

ALSO SEE MAPS ON PAGES 60 • 101

TO HWY 89A

RED HILLS
to OAK CREEK

Hikes 45–49
Red Rock State Park
4050 Lower Red Rock Loop Road

Red Rock State Park is a 286-acre nature preserve and environmental education center with exhibits, programs, and ranger-led hikes. The state park, surrounded by red sandstone buttes and mesas, is located just south of Scheurman Mountain and downstream from Crescent Moon Ranch at an elevation of 3,900 feet. The state park was originally part of the Smoke Trail Ranch, owned by Jack and Helen Frye and opened to the public in 1991. Serpentine Oak Creek meanders 1.5 miles through the park, creating a diverse ecosystem and a lush riparian corridor with cottonwoods, sycamores, and willows. The arid hillside slopes and mesas are covered with live oak, manzanita, pinyon pine, juniper, and low-growing cactus.

The state park has a 6-mile network of ten interlinking hiking trails, including a handicapped-accessible path. The well-groomed trails follow the banks of Oak Creek and lead through green meadows, stream-fed canyons, across ridges and scenic bluffs, and up red sandstone hills to overlooks. Eagles' Nest, at 4,102 feet, is the highest point in the state park. The vistas from atop the summit are stunning.

The five hikes included here begin from the Red Rock State Park Visitor Center and loop through this gorgeous park, exploring a wide cross section of Sedona's natural wonders.

Driving directions: From the Sedona Y (Highways 89A and 179 junction), drive 5.5 miles southwest on Highway 89A (towards Cottonwood) to Lower Red Rock Loop Road. Turn left and drive 3 miles to the Red Rock State Park turnoff on the right. Turn right and continue 0.6 miles, passing the entrance station to the visitor center parking lot. An entrance fee is required.

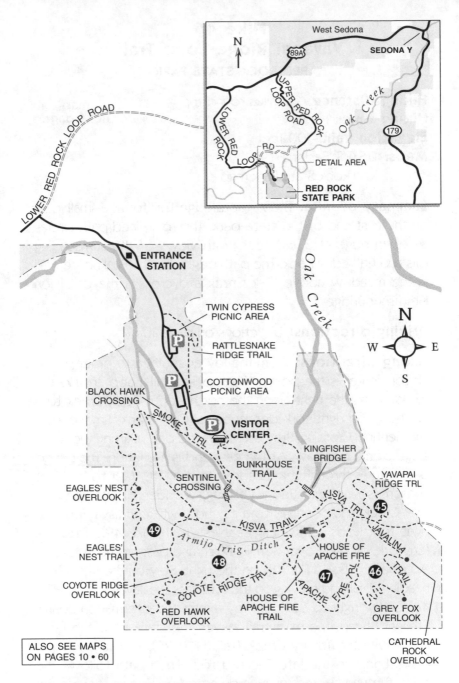

RED ROCK STATE PARK

Hike 45
Yavapai Ridge Loop Trail
RED ROCK STATE PARK

Hiking distance: 1.5 miles round trip
Hiking time: 1 hour
Elevation gain: 100 feet
Maps: U.S.G.S. Sedona
      Red Rock State Park map

map
next page

Summary of hike: The Yavapai Ridge Trail forms a small loop on the east end of the state park. The rock-lined path circles an open ridge at 3,950 feet, with views of the surrounding hills and Cathedral Rock. The path begins on the Bunkhouse Trail in the meadow above Oak Creek and crosses the creek on Kingfisher Bridge.

Driving directions: Directions on page 104.

Hiking directions: From the lower southeast corner of the visitor center is the posted Bunkhouse Trail. Loop around the meadow to the right along the north side of Oak Creek to a junction. The right fork descends to Oak Creek, Smoke Trail, and Sentinel Crossing. Stay on the paved path, skirting the south edge of the meadow. At the east end is a junction. The paved path returns through the meadow to the left. Veer to the right and cross Kingfisher Bridge, a long, wooden bridge spanning Oak Creek, and continue to a junction with the Kisva Trail. The right fork leads to the Eagles' Nest Trail (Hike 49). Take the left fork, crossing over Armijo Ditch and passing the House of Apache Fire Trail (Hike 48) on the right. Stay on the Kisva Trail, heading uphill and curving to the left. Pass the Javalina Trail (Hike 46) on the right to a junction by a map and information board. Straight ahead, the main trail leaves the state park and connects with the Turkey Creek Trail (Hike 96). Take the Yavapai Ridge Loop to the left. The red rock-lined path follows the ridge through cypress groves on a downhill slope. Across the canyon, homes line the top of the bluffs. Loop back to the left and cross over the ridge. Complete the loop at the Kisva Trail, across from the Javalina Trail. Return by retracing your steps.

Hike 46
Javalina—Apache Fire Trail Loop
RED ROCK STATE PARK

Hiking distance: 2 mile loop
Hiking time: 1 hour
Elevation gain: 100 feet
Maps: U.S.G.S. Sedona
   Red Rock State Park map

*map
next page*

Summary of hike: The Javalina Trail and Apache Fire Trail loop through the upper slopes of the state park through a pinyon pine and juniper woodland. The trail begins on the Bunkhouse Trail in the meadow above Oak Creek and leaves the meadow, crossing the creek on Kingfisher Bridge. The Kisva Trail climbs to the east end of the state park and is a connector route for both trails.

Driving directions: Directions on page 104.

Hiking directions: Follow the hiking directions of Hike 45 to Kingfisher Bridge. Cross the long, wooden bridge over Oak Creek to a junction with the Kisva Trail. The right fork leads to the Eagles' Nest Trail (Hike 49). Take the left fork, crossing over Armijo Ditch and passing the House of Apache Fire Trail (Hike 48) on the right. Stay on the Kisva Trail, and head uphill to the Javalina Trail on the right. Bear right and follow the red rock-lined path uphill to the ridge. Follow the ridge overlooking House Mountain to the south; Wilson Mountain and Capitol Butte lie to the north. Make a horseshoe left bend and cross over the ridge to the southern slope and an overlook of Cathedral Rock. Continue to the right, leaving the ridge to a junction with the Grey Fox Overlook. Detour left a short distance to an overlook with a bench. Return to the Javalina Trail, and zigzag down to the canyon floor. Cross a seasonal drainage to a junction with the Apache Fire Trail. Take the right fork and continue down the west slope of the canyon, completing the loop at a junction with the Kisva Trail. Return to the left.

Hike 47
Apache Fire Trail Loop
RED ROCK STATE PARK

Hiking distance: 1.7 mile loop
Hiking time: 1 hour
Elevation gain: 100 feet
Maps: U.S.G.S. Sedona
　　　　Red Rock State Park map

Summary of hike: The Apache Fire Trail was named for the Yavapai–Apache Indians who camped along Oak Creek during the construction of the House of Apache Fire in the late 1940s. Smoke from their campfires led to the name. The Apache Fire Trail loops around the historic pueblo-style mansion with views of the beautiful waterways and surrounding formations, including a dramatic view of Cathedral Rock's west face. The hike begins in the meadow southeast of the visitor center and crosses the creek on Kingfisher Bridge.

Driving directions: Directions on page 104.

Hiking directions: Follow the hiking directions of Hike 45 to Kingfisher Bridge. Cross the long, wooden bridge over Oak Creek to a junction with the Kisva Trail. The right fork leads to the Eagles' Nest Trail (Hike 49 and the return route). Take the left fork, crossing over Armijo Ditch to the House of Apache Fire Trail on the right. Continue a short distance on the Kisva Trail to the Apache Fire Trail. Bear right up the rock steps, and traverse the east-facing slope in a small red rock canyon. Drop down to the canyon floor and cross a drainage to a posted junction. To the left is the Javalina Trail (Hike 46). Curve right, staying on the Apache Fire Trail. Recross the drainage and continue on the gentle uphill grade to a junction. Detour to the right to visit the gated House of Apache Fire, a red rock house built in 1947 but never completed. Just beyond the house is a magnificent overlook of Cathedral Rock and the mountains surrounding Sedona. Return to the junction and continue on the hillside to a trail split, across the canyon from the House of Apache Fire. Take the right fork and descend down hill to the Kisva Trail at Oak Creek. Follow the creek to the right to Kingfisher Bridge. Cross the bridge and return to the visitor center.

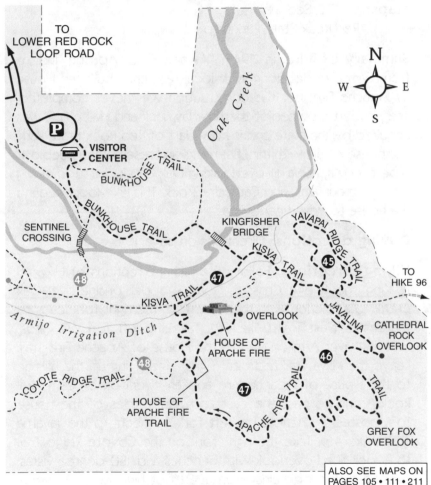

HIKES 45–47
RED ROCK STATE PARK

Hike 48
House of Apache Fire —
Coyote Ridge Loop Trail
RED ROCK STATE PARK

Hiking distance: 2 mile loop
Hiking time: 1 hour
Elevation gain: 100 feet
Maps: U.S.G.S. Sedona
      Red Rock State Park map

Summary of hike: In 1947, Yavapai and Apache Indians from Camp Verde, along with local residents, built the House of Apache Fire, but the construction was never completed. The property, owned at the time by Jack and Helen Fry, was acquired by the state and is now part of Red Rock State Park. The house is built with thin, flat rocks and resembles a pueblo. It is perched high on a hill overlooking Oak Creek, the surrounding redrock mountains, and Cathedral Rock. This hike loops around the house to magnificent vistas.

Driving directions: Directions on page 104.

Hiking directions: Follow the hiking directions of Hike 45 to Kingfisher Bridge. Cross the long, wooden bridge over Oak Creek to a junction with the Kisva Trail. The right fork leads to the Eagles' Nest Trail (Hike 49). Take the left fork 60 yards, crossing over Armijo Ditch to the House of Apache Fire Trail. Leave the Kisva Trail and bear right, zigzagging up the hillside to the House of Apache Fire and an overlook of Cathedral Rock. Continue past the east and south sides of the house to a posted T-junction. The left fork connects to the Javalina Trail (Hike 46). Take the right fork on the Coyote Ridge Trail to a rock-lined overlook with benches and 180-degree vistas. Cross a slick rock drainage on a 12-foot-high ledge. Traverse the hillside to a trail split, across the canyon from the House of Apache Fire. Continue straight (on the left fork) and traverse the north-facing hillside to a Y-fork. The left fork leads to Eagles' Nest (Hike 49). Veer right and descend, passing the Coyote Ridge Overlook on the right. Three short switchbacks drop down the draw to a junction with the Kisva Trail at Oak Creek. Bear right and stroll along Oak Creek through lush riparian habitat to the Sentinel Bridge junction. Bear left on the sandy path, and cross a series of three wooden bridges. Climb up to the paved Bunkhouse Trail and return to the left.

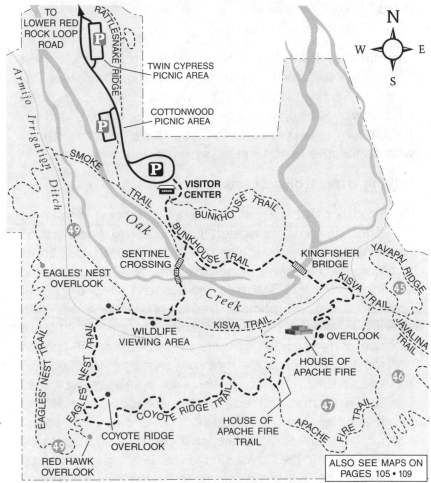

HOUSE OF APACHE FIRE–
COYOTE RIDGE
RED ROCK STATE PARK

Hike 49
Eagles' Nest Loop Trail
RED ROCK STATE PARK

Hiking distance: 2 mile loop
Hiking time: 1 hour
Elevation gain: 200 feet
Maps: U.S.G.S. Sedona
      Red Rock State Park map

Summary of hike: Eagles' Nest, at 4,102 feet, is the highest point in the state park. The route to the summit crosses Oak Creek on Sentinel Bridge and follows the creek downstream through groves of sycamores, cottonwoods, willows, and ash. The path zigzags up the north-facing slope to the overlook with interpretive panels and sweeping 360-degree vistas.

Driving directions: Directions on page 104.

Hiking directions: From the lower southeast corner of the visitor center is the posted Bunkhouse Trail. Loop around the meadow to the right along the north side of Oak Creek to a junction. The paved Bunkhouse Trail continues along the meadow to the left. Bear right and descend to Oak Creek at Sentinel Crossing. The Smoke Trail continues along the north bank of the creek. Cross Sentinel Bridge on a series of three wooden bridges, and follow the sandy path to a T-junction with the Kisva Trail. Take the right fork, passing a wildlife viewing bench on the left to a junction with the Eagles' Nest Trail. Bear left along the east edge of the meadow, and ascend the hillside. Near the top, three short switchbacks lead to the Coyote Ridge Overlook on the left. Continue a short distance to a junction with the Coyote Ridge Trail. Bear right, staying on the Eagles' Nest Trail, and zigzag up to the Red Hawk Overlook on the left. Detour a short distance to the overlook with vistas to the north and east. Continue on the main trail, curving around a gully and following the ridge. Skirt the west boundary of the state park, and head uphill to the Eagles' Nest Overlook on the right. From the 4,102-foot summit are stunning vistas. After marveling at the sights, descend on the winding path, crossing a bridge over Armijo Ditch to the Kisva Trail at Black Hawk Crossing. Take the Kisva Trail to the right, and stroll along Oak Creek through lush riparian habitat back to the Sentinel Bridge junction. Cross the bridges and retrace your steps to the visitor center.

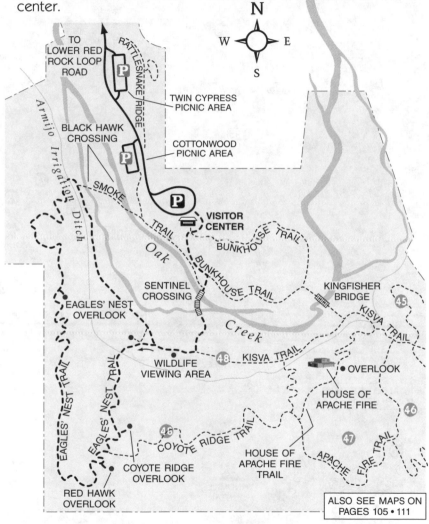

EAGLES' NEST TRAIL
RED ROCK STATE PARK

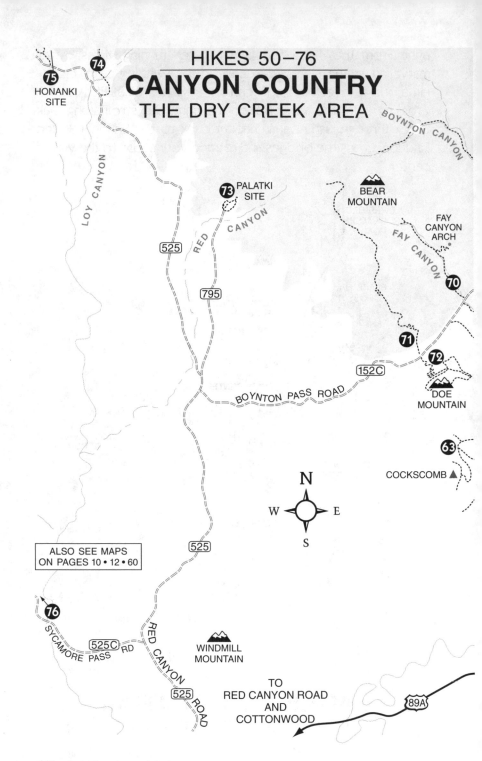

HIKES 50–76
CANYON COUNTRY
THE DRY CREEK AREA

BOYNTON CANYON

75 HONANKI SITE

74

LOY CANYON

73 PALATKI SITE

BEAR MOUNTAIN

FAY CANYON ARCH

FAY CANYON

RED CANYON

525

795

70

71

79

152C

BOYNTON PASS ROAD

DOE MOUNTAIN

63

COCKSCOMB ▲

N
W ◆ E
S

ALSO SEE MAPS
ON PAGES 10 • 12 • 60

525

76

SYCAMORE PASS RD

525C

RED CANYON ROAD

WINDMILL MOUNTAIN

525 ROAD

TO
RED CANYON ROAD
AND
COTTONWOOD

89A

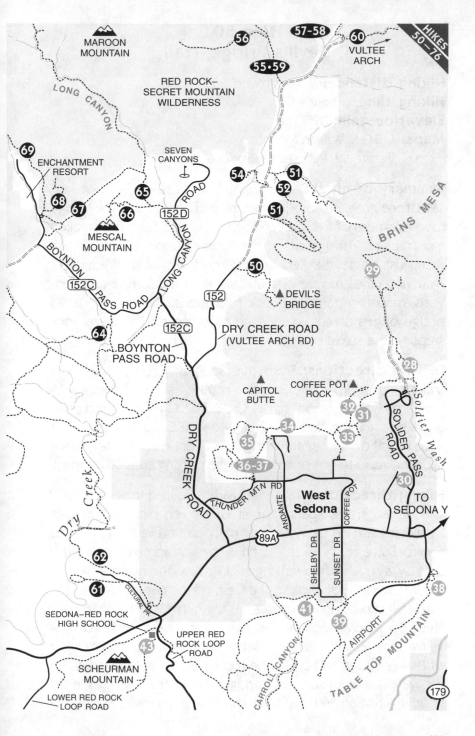

MAROON
MOUNTAIN

56

57-58

60

VULTEE
ARCH

55•59

RED ROCK–
SECRET MOUNTAIN
WILDERNESS

LONG CANYON

BRINS MESA

69

ENCHANTMENT
RESORT

SEVEN
CANYONS

54

51

52

51

68

67

65

LONG CANYON ROAD

152 D

66

MESCAL
MOUNTAIN

29

152C

BOYNTON PASS ROAD

LONG CANYON ROAD

152

50

DEVIL'S
BRIDGE

64

152C

BOYNTON
PASS ROAD

DRY CREEK ROAD
(VULTEE ARCH RD)

28

CAPITOL
BUTTE

COFFEE POT
ROCK

Soldier Wash

32

31

34

33

35

SOLIDER PASS ROAD

DRY CREEK ROAD

36-37

THUNDER MTN RD

West
Sedona

COFFEE POT

30

TO
SEDONA Y

Dry Creek

62

ANDANTE

89A

SHELBY DR

SUNSET DR

38

61

SEDONA–RED ROCK
HIGH SCHOOL

CULTURAL PK

41

39

AIRPORT

43

UPPER RED
ROCK LOOP
ROAD

CARROLL CANYON

TABLE TOP MOUNTAIN

SCHEURMAN
MOUNTAIN

LOWER RED ROCK
LOOP ROAD

179

100 Great Hikes - **115**

Hike 50
Devil's Bridge Trail

Hiking distance: 2 miles round trip
Hiking time: 1 hour
Elevation gain: 320 feet
Maps: U.S.G.S. Wilson Mountain
        Beartooth Publishing—Sedona, AZ

Summary of hike: Devil's Bridge, a massive 54-foot-high sandstone arch, is the tallest natural arch in Sedona. The bridge has a thickness of five feet and spans over 45 feet. The cracked and fractured bridge sits at the foot of Capitol Butte's north face, just inside the Red Rock—Secret Mountain Wilderness. From atop the arch are dramatic vistas of the surrounding canyons, mountains, and red rock formations. The trail to Devil's bridge begins on an old unpaved road and climbs natural rock steps to the summit.

Driving directions: From the Sedona Y (Highways 89A and 179 junction), drive 3.1 miles southwest on Highway 89A (towards Cottonwood) to Dry Creek Road. Turn right and drive 2 miles to the posted Dry Creek Road (F.S. Road 152/Vultee Arch Road) on the right. Turn right and continue 1.3 miles on the unpaved road to the posted trailhead parking area on the right.

Hiking directions: Take the wide, posted trail east, and wind through the sparse forest of pinyon pine and juniper. Parallel a wash on the near-level path, and curve right towards Capitol Butte at 0.4 miles. Continue strolling up canyon to a trail split by a huge rock overhang at 0.7 miles. The narrow path to the left leads 100 yards to the base of the natural bridge. The main trail curves right and ascends the cliff face on steep rock steps to an overlook of the surrounding basin and red rock formations. Head up another set of rock steps to the backside of Devil's Bridge and up to the top of the arch. Numerous hikers walk out on the unstable bridge. Due to the fractures in the rock, it is not advisable. To return, retrace your steps.

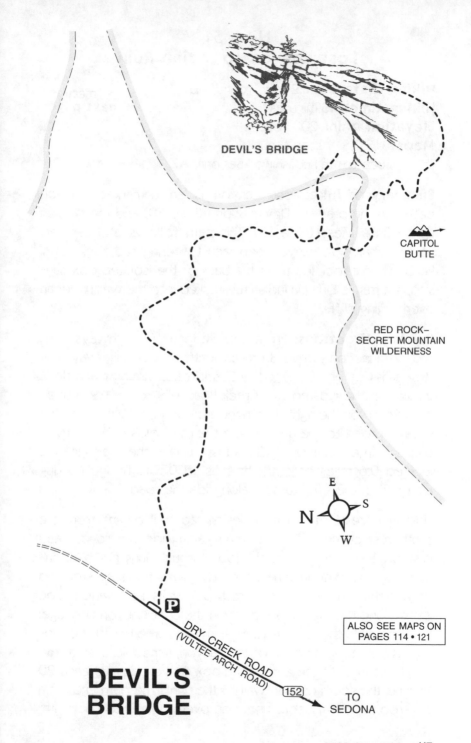

DEVIL'S BRIDGE

CAPITOL
BUTTE

RED ROCK–
SECRET MOUNTAIN
WILDERNESS

E
N   S
W

ALSO SEE MAPS ON
PAGES 114 • 121

DRY CREEK ROAD
(VULTEE ARCH ROAD)
152

TO
SEDONA

DEVIL'S
BRIDGE

Hike 51
Lost Canyon to Indian Ruin

Hiking distance: 1.2 miles round trip
Hiking time: 45 minutes
Elevation gain: 200 feet
Maps: U.S.G.S. Wilson Mountain
Beartooth Publishing—Sedona, AZ

map
next page

Summary of hike: Lost Canyon is an unmarked canyon between the draw to Devil's Bridge (Hike 50) and the canyon up to Brins Mesa (Hike 53). This path follows a streambed up the small side canyon between towering red rock cliffs. Perched on a rock ledge, at the back of the isolated box canyon, is a fragile Sinagua Indian ruin tucked into the wall under an overhanging cliff.

Driving directions: From the Sedona Y (Highways 89A and 179 junction), drive 3.1 miles southwest on Highway 89A (towards Cottonwood) to Dry Creek Road. Turn right and drive 2 miles to the posted Dry Creek Road (F.S. Road 152/Vultee Arch Road) on the right. Turn right and continue 1.9 miles on the unpaved road to the area where the road dips into a canyon drainage. The unmarked trailhead is found in the drainage. It is located 0.6 miles beyond the posted Devil's Bridge parking area. Park in the small turnout alongside the road.

Hiking directions: The undesignated trail begins from the southwest corner of the drainage alongside the road. Head east up the red slick rock floor through junipers, Arizona cypress, and pinyon pines. Steadily climb the stair-stepped draw between the towering red rock walls. Pass various side paths along the way. Stay mainly in the Lost Canyon drainage, but a path on the left wall will eliminate some boulder climbing. As you near the back of the canyon, scramble over a few deadfall trees. At the end of the box canyon, a path leads 20 feet up the south canyon wall to the right. The path ends at a one-room Indian pueblo under an overhanging red rock cliff.

Under the overhang is an awesome spot with a mesmerizing view of the vertical-walled cirque.

Hike 52
Lost Canyon Cliffside Trail
to an Indian ruin overlook and
Devil's Bridge Overlook

Hiking distance: 4 miles round trip
Hiking time: 2 hours
Elevation gain: 800 feet
Maps: U.S.G.S. Wilson Mountain
      Beartooth Publishing—Sedona, AZ

map next page

Summary of hike: Lost Canyon is an unmarked canyon between the draw to Devil's Bridge (Hike 50) and the canyon up to Brins Mesa (Hike 53). Hike 51 follows the Lost Canyon floor between towering red rock cliffs to a Sinagua Indian ruin at the back of the box canyon. This hike begins on the west end of the Brins Mesa Trail and steeply climbs the south wall to the cliff-hugging trail in Lost Canyon, high above the ruin. The path loops through two canyons on a narrow cliffside ledge, overlooking two Indian ruins and offering a unique view of Devil's Bridge.

Driving directions: From the Sedona Y (Highways 89A and 179 junction), drive 3.1 miles southwest on Highway 89A (towards Cottonwood) to Dry Creek Road. Turn right and drive 2 miles to the posted Dry Creek Road (F.S. Road 152/Vultee Arch Road) on the right. Turn right and continue 2.5 miles on the unpaved road to the posted Brins Mesa parking area on the right.

Hiking directions: Head east on the posted Brins Mesa Trail. At 60 yards, leave the main trail and take the unsigned footpath to the right. (From the junction, the trailhead information board can still be seen.) Go to the right and cross a rocky wash. Continue south up and over a small hill to a slick rock wash with a sweeping view across the Dry Creek Basin. Curve east up the wash, and begin a steep, goat-like ascent on the rocky trail to an overhanging red rock formation. Bear left, curving clockwise around the formation to the summit. The path levels out and crosses the forested plateau toward the prominent red rock butte at the north tip of Lost Canyon. Curve around the monolith into the sheer-walled canyon, rising a thousand feet above the valley floor. Traverse the vertical north canyon wall perched on the edge of the cliff. An Indian pueblo can be spotted halfway up the cliff on the north canyon wall. Continue east, overlooking another well-preserved Indian ruin at the upper end of the canyon floor. Loop around to Lost Canyon's south side, crossing high above the ruin and passing a fissure. Wind through the forested north-facing slope, close to the edge of the sheer wall. Loop around the southwest tip of Lost Canyon along the eroding cliffs. Curve left into the canyon with Devil's Bridge, where there is an eye-level view across the canyon of the natural arch on the north face of Capitol Butte. This is the turn-around spot. Return along the same route.

SINAGUA INDIAN RUIN

HIKES 51 • 52
LOST CANYON
TO INDIAN RUIN • DEVIL'S BRIDGE
OVERLOOK

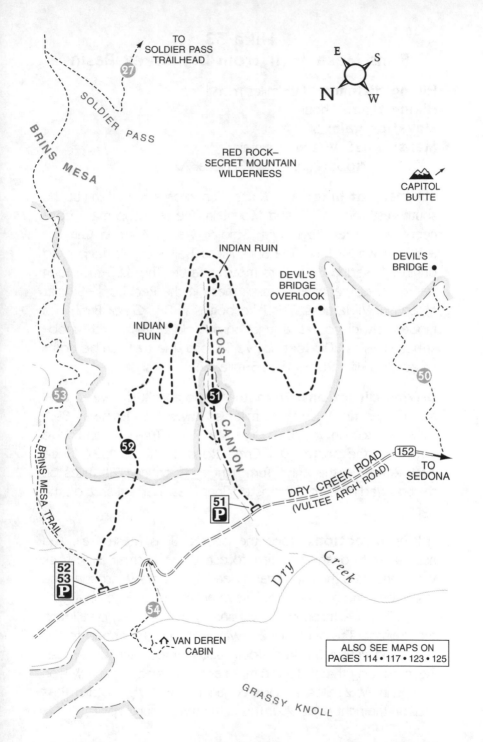

TO
SOLDIER PASS
TRAILHEAD

27

SOLDIER PASS

BRINS MESA

E
S
N
W

RED ROCK–
SECRET MOUNTAIN
WILDERNESS

CAPITOL
BUTTE

INDIAN RUIN

DEVIL'S
BRIDGE
OVERLOOK

DEVIL'S
BRIDGE ●

INDIAN ●
RUIN

LOST

53

CANYON

52

51

50

BRINS MESA TRAIL

DRY CREEK ROAD
(VULTEE ARCH ROAD)

152

TO
SEDONA

51
P

52
53
P

Dry   Creek

54

VAN DEREN
CABIN

ALSO SEE MAPS ON
PAGES 114 • 117 • 123 • 125

GRASSY KNOLL

Hike 53
Brins Mesa Trail from Dry Creek Basin

Hiking distance: 4.25 miles round trip
Hiking time: 2 hours
Elevation gain: 500 feet
Maps: U.S.G.S. Wilson Mountain
       Beartooth Publishing—Sedona, AZ

Summary of hike: Brins Mesa is an expansive plateau at the southwest foot of Wilson Mountain. The tabletop mesa connects Dry Creek Basin with Soldier Wash, Mormon Canyon, and Uptown Sedona. The Brins Mesa Trail is an old jeep road originally used by ranchers moving cattle. The 4.25-mile-long trail crosses the open, grassy mesa in the Red Rock—Secret Mountain Wilderness. This hike begins in Dry Creek Basin and moderately climbs to a junction at Soldier Pass, with unobstructed vistas 800 feet above Sedona. The trail can be combined with Hike 26 for a 4.25-mile, one-way shuttle.

Driving directions: From the Sedona Y (Highways 89A and 179 junction), drive 3.1 miles southwest on Highway 89A (towards Cottonwood) to Dry Creek Road. Turn right and drive 2 miles to the posted Dry Creek Road (F.S. Road 152/Vultee Arch Road) on the right. Turn right and continue 2.5 miles on the unpaved road to the posted Brins Mesa parking area on the right.

Hiking directions: Take the posted Brins Mesa Trail, and head east through an open forest. Cross a small slick rock wash, and pass through a gate. Head up the draw, crossing the streambed and red slick rock several times. Continue on a gentle uphill grade through an Arizona cypress forest, parallel to the drainage. The path moves away from the streambed to the south and enters the Red Rock—Secret Mountain Wilderness. Begin climbing the hill to the mesa as views open up to Wilson Mountain. At 2 miles is a posted junction with the Soldier Pass Trail on the right (Hike 29). This is the turn-around spot.

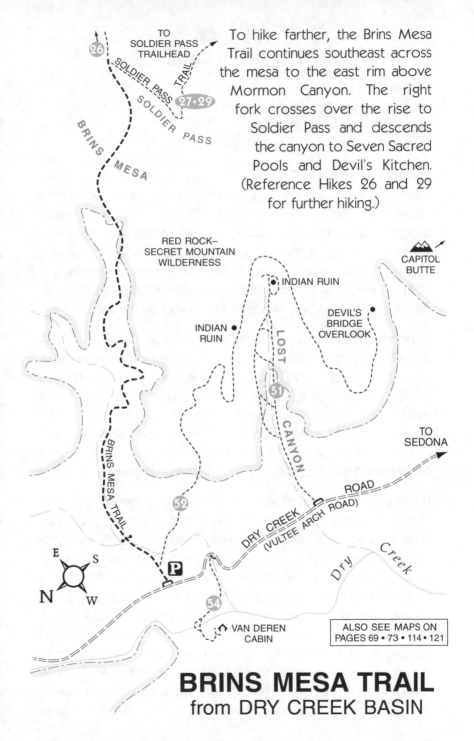

To hike farther, the Brins Mesa Trail continues southeast across the mesa to the east rim above Mormon Canyon. The right fork crosses over the rise to Soldier Pass and descends the canyon to Seven Sacred Pools and Devil's Kitchen. (Reference Hikes 26 and 29 for further hiking.)

TO SOLDIER PASS TRAILHEAD

26

SOLDIER PASS TRAIL

27·29

SOLDIER PASS

BRINS MESA

RED ROCK–
SECRET MOUNTAIN
WILDERNESS

CAPITOL BUTTE

INDIAN RUIN

DEVIL'S BRIDGE OVERLOOK

INDIAN RUIN

LOST CANYON

51

TO SEDONA

BRINS MESA TRAIL

52

DRY CREEK ROAD
(VULTEE ARCH ROAD)

Dry Creek

E S

N W

P

54

VAN DEREN CABIN

ALSO SEE MAPS ON
PAGES 69 • 73 • 114 • 121

BRINS MESA TRAIL
from DRY CREEK BASIN

Hike 54
Van Deren Cabin

Hiking distance: 1 mile round trip
Hiking time: 30 minutes
Elevation gain: 200 feet
Maps: U.S.G.S. Wilson Mountain

Summary of hike: The historic Van Deren Cabin is comprised of two hand-hewn log cabins joined together with a metal roof. Earl Van Deren, who homesteaded the acreage, built the two one-room cabins, including a red rock fireplace, in the 1890s. Although the cabin site is surrounded by private ranchland, the cabin is owned by the Forest Service and is open to the public. Jeep tours regularly visit the cabin. This was the site for the Robert Mitchum film Blood on the Moon.

Driving directions: From the Sedona Y (Highways 89A and 179 junction), drive 3.1 miles southwest on Highway 89A (towards Cottonwood) to Dry Creek Road. Turn right and drive 2 miles to the posted Dry Creek Road (F.S. Road 152/Vultee Arch Road) on the right. Turn right and continue 2.4 miles on the unpaved road to a distinct but unmarked jeep road on the left. Park in a pullout along Dry Creek Road. The pullout is 0.1 miles before reaching the posted Brins Mesa parking area.

Hiking directions: Walk downhill on the forested jeep road. (The narrow road can also be driven, but it is easier and more enjoyable to walk from Dry Creek Road.) Gradually descend the draw, with views of the red rock formations across the basin. At 0.3 miles, the unpaved road reaches Dry Creek in a beautiful red slick rock area. When the creek is running, cross to the right of the road on the water-carved red rock ledge. The sculpted waterway is filled with water chutes and small pools—it is a great area to explore. Pick up the old road across the creek, and head uphill to a trail split. The right fork climbs to a sloping slick rock draw. Take the left fork, curving to a scenic overlook on a rocky ledge above the creek. The 360-degree vistas include Wilson Mountain, Lost Mountain, and Secret Mountain. Continue northwest 50 yards to the Van Deren Cabin, an old log structure with a red rock foundation adjacent to Grassy Knolls. Return along the same route.

GRASSY KNOLLS
4,873' • 4,872'

VAN DEREN CABIN

Dry Creek

W

S ✦ N

E

TO
SEDONA

[152]

DRY CREEK ROAD
(VULTEE ARCH ROAD)

P

BRINS MESA TRAIL

ALSO SEE MAPS ON
PAGES 114 • 123

VAN DEREN
CABIN

TO
LOST CANYON

52

53

TO
SOLDIER
PASS

Hike 55
Secret Canyon Trail

Hiking distance: 5 miles round trip
Hiking time: 2.5 hours
Elevation gain: 600 feet
Maps: U.S.G.S. Wilson Mountain
       Beartooth Publishing—Sedona, AZ

map
next page

Summary of hike: Secret Canyon is a long and remote canyon that begins in the Dry Creek Basin and immediately enters the Red Rock—Secret Mountain Wilderness. The trail follows the canyon floor, with open vistas of Dry Creek Basin, then explores the scenic red rock country beneath Maroon Mountain, Secret Mountain, and the Mogollon Rim. In the upper canyon, a fortress of vertical red rock walls rise more than 2,000 feet above the trail.

Driving directions: From the Sedona Y (Highways 89A and 179 junction), drive 3.1 miles southwest on Highway 89A (towards Cottonwood) to Dry Creek Road. Turn right and drive 2 miles to the posted Dry Creek Road (F.S. Road 152/Vultee Arch Road) on the right. Turn right and continue 3.4 miles to the posted trailhead parking area on the left.

Hiking directions: From the back end of the parking area, cross the dry streambed on the Secret Canyon Trail, and enter the Red Rock—Secret Mountain Wilderness. The level path winds through a forest of pine, sycamore, cottonwood, and juniper surrounded by eroding red rock formations. Parallel the east side of the streambed (which flows during the winter and spring) into the mouth of the wide, red-walled canyon. Cross the streambed and go 40 yards to the posted HS Canyon Trail on the left at 0.6 miles (Hike 56). Continue straight ahead on the right fork, staying in Secret Canyon through groves of manzanita. Cross two narrow slick rock drainages, and continue slightly uphill along the east side of Maroon Mountain, surrounded by magnificent sandstone formations. Descend and cross a drainage, curving to the left and then right. Drop down into a shady oak and cypress grove at a posted junction with the David Miller Trail on the right at 1.7 miles (Hike 59). Curve left and cross a slick rock drainage, staying in the main drainage of Secret Canyon. Head west and drop down the north wall of the tree-filled canyon, overlooking the water-carved, red rock canyon. Enter a pine forest beneath the vertical red cliffs, and slowly descend to the creek. Cross the creek to a flat grassy meadow with towering pines and Gambel oaks. This is a great spot to stop and enjoy the surroundings.

To hike farther, the trail winds up the canyon for two more miles, with frequent stream crossings and pools. The trail fades near the back (west) end of the canyon.

Hike 56
HS Canyon Trail

Hiking distance: 5 miles round trip
Hiking time: 2.5 hours
Elevation gain: 800 feet
Maps: U.S.G.S. Wilson Mountain
       Beartooth Publishing—Sedona, AZ

map
next page

Summary of hike: HS Canyon is a scenic side canyon branching off from Secret Canyon. The box canyon winds into a narrow pocket on the east slope of Maroon Mountain in the Red Rock–Secret Mountain Wilderness. The intimate canyon path climbs in the shade of oaks and alligator junipers, surrounded by red rock formations and 1,000-foot-high cliffs. The hike follows the Secret Canyon Trail for the first 0.6 miles and ends at the back of HS Canyon along the sheer vertical face of Maroon Mountain.

Driving directions: From the Sedona Y (Highways 89A and 179 junction), drive 3.1 miles southwest on Highway 89A (towards Cottonwood) to Dry Creek Road. Turn right and drive 2 miles to the posted Dry Creek Road (F.S. Road 152/Vultee

Arch Road) on the right. Turn right and continue 3.4 miles to the posted Secret Canyon trailhead parking area on the left.

Hiking directions: From the back end of the parking area, cross the dry streambed on the Secret Canyon Trail, and enter the Red Rock–Secret Mountain Wilderness. The level path winds through a pine and juniper forest surrounded by eroding red rock formations. Parallel the east side of the streambed (which flows during the winter and spring) into the mouth of the wide, red-walled canyon. Cross the streambed and go 40 yards to the posted HS Canyon Trail on the left at 0.6 miles. Leave Secret Canyon and take the left fork. Gradually climb through the oak and alligator juniper forest as the trail dips and rises. Parallel a slick rock draw, and head towards the east face of Maroon Mountain. As the canyon narrows, continue heading towards the jagged canyon rim, reaching the 6,200-foot fin on Maroon Mountain. Follow the south edge of the canyon alongside the drainage to the base of the prominent vertical wall. Curve right to the north face of the wall, entering a narrow pocket canyon with moss-covered rocks and colorful lichen. Zigzag across the drainage, and climb the canyon's northern hillside. The trail ends near the back of the box canyon, surrounded by the sheer walls of Maroon Mountain.

HIKE 55
SECRET CANYON
HIKE 56
HS CANYON

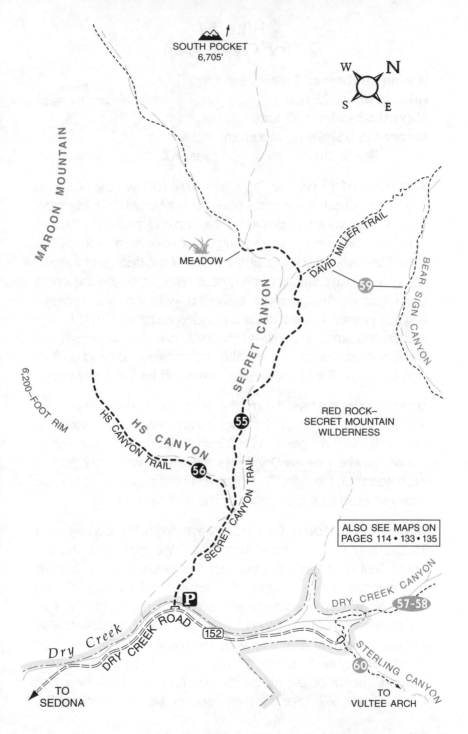

SOUTH POCKET
6,705'

N
W   E
S

MAROON MOUNTAIN

MEADOW

DAVID MILLER TRAIL

59

BEAR SIGN CANYON

SECRET CANYON

6,200-FOOT RIM

HS CANYON

HS CANYON TRAIL

56

55

SECRET CANYON TRAIL

RED ROCK–
SECRET MOUNTAIN
WILDERNESS

ALSO SEE MAPS ON
PAGES 114 • 133 • 135

DRY CREEK CANYON

57-58

P

Dry Creek

DRY CREEK ROAD

152

STERLING CANYON

60

TO
SEDONA

TO
VULTEE ARCH

Hike 57
Dry Creek Trail

Hiking distance: 5 miles round trip
Hiking time: 2.5 hours
Elevation gain: 450 feet
Maps: U.S.G.S. Wilson Mountain
      Beartooth Publishing—Sedona, AZ

map
next page

Summary of hike: The Dry Creek Trail follows the headwaters of Dry Creek in the Red Rock–Secret Mountain Wilderness. The creek flows south down the canyon and meanders through Dry Creek Basin, eventually joining Oak Creek west of Red Rock State Park. This trail begins at the head of the basin and follows the creek upstream deep into the canyon, crossing the creek several times. The canyon is shaded with Arizona cypress, alligator juniper, Douglas fir, and ponderosa pine, with lush vegetation and small grottos. When Dry Creek is running high, the trail is not recommended. An alternative hike is to head up Bear Sign Canyon (Hike 58), which branches off to the northwest.

Driving directions: From the Sedona Y (Highways 89A and 179 junction), drive 3.1 miles southwest on Highway 89A (towards Cottonwood) to Dry Creek Road. Turn right and drive 2 miles to the posted Dry Creek Road (F.S. Road 152/Vultee Arch Road) on the right. Turn right and continue 4.3 miles on the unpaved road to the trailhead at the end of the road.

Hiking directions: Two trails leave from the parking area. To the east is the Vultee Arch Trail (Hike 60). Take the Dry Creek Trail on the north and cross the wash. Cross Dry Creek to the mouth of the canyon, and enter the Red Rock–Secret Mountain Wilderness. Follow the sandy path through the forest on the west side of the canyon beneath East Pocket. Walk through a narrow drainage with overhanging red rock walls. Cross Dry Creek two times to a posted Y-fork where two canyons merge at 0.7 miles. The left fork heads up Bear Sign Canyon (Hike 59). Take the right fork up the west bank of Dry

Creek, following the creek under the shadow of the surrounding red rock buttes and cliffs. At 1.4 miles, a side canyon veers off to the right. Cross the streambed to the left. At 2 miles the path intersects another streambed and a perpendicular trail running east and west. This is a good turn-around spot. To hike farther, the trail fades and involves boulder scrambling.

Hike 58
Bear Sign Trail

Hiking distance: 7.6 miles round trip
Hiking time: 4 hours
Elevation gain: 600 feet
Maps: U.S.G.S. Wilson Mountain
      Beartooth Publishing—Sedona, AZ

map next page

Summary of hike: Bear Sign Canyon is a quiet, intimate canyon within the Red Rock—Secret Mountain Wilderness. The shady, remote canyon has gorgeous rock formations that rise hundreds of feet above the canyon floor. The hike begins on the Dry Creek Trail and veers west into Bear Sign Canyon, winding through groves of sycamore, cottonwood, Arizona cypress, Douglas fir, and ponderosa pine. The trail ends at the base of the Mogollon Rim in a fern-covered alcove beneath the towering cliffs of coconino sandstone.

Driving directions: From the Sedona Y (Highways 89A and 179 junction), drive 3.1 miles southwest on Highway 89A (towards Cottonwood) to Dry Creek Road. Turn right and drive 2 miles to the posted Dry Creek Road (F.S. Road 152/Vultee Arch Road) on the right. Turn right and continue 4.3 miles on the unpaved road to the trailhead at the end of the road.

Hiking directions: Two trails leave from the parking area. To the east is the Vultee Arch Trail (Hike 60). Take the Dry Creek Trail on the north and cross the wash. Cross Dry Creek to the mouth of the canyon, entering the Red Rock—Secret Mountain Wilderness. Follow the sandy path through the forest on the west side of the canyon beneath East Pocket. Walk through a narrow drainage with overhanging red sandstone walls. Cross Dry Creek two times to a posted Y-fork where two canyons merge at 0.7 miles. The right fork heads up Dry Creek Canyon (Hike 57). Take the left fork and cross the streambed (or rock-hop when the creek is flowing) into Bear Sign Canyon. Continue through a narrow red-walled wash. Climb out and meander through a forest on a gently sloping grade. The trail maintains an easy grade through a narrow canyon that parallels the drainage. As you near the massive south-facing mountain wall, curve left and head west. Traverse the shady north-facing slope, over-looking the rock gorge. Cross the drainage numerous times to a posted junction on the left at 2.5 miles. The David Miller Trail climbs the west canyon wall and connects with Secret Canyon (Hike 59). Stay on the main trail, steadily gaining elevation while perched on the west canyon wall. One mile past the junction, at the back of the canyon, the trail ends on the canyon floor surrounded by towering trees and cliffs.

HIKE 57
DRY CREEK TRAIL
HIKE 58
BEAR SIGN TRAIL

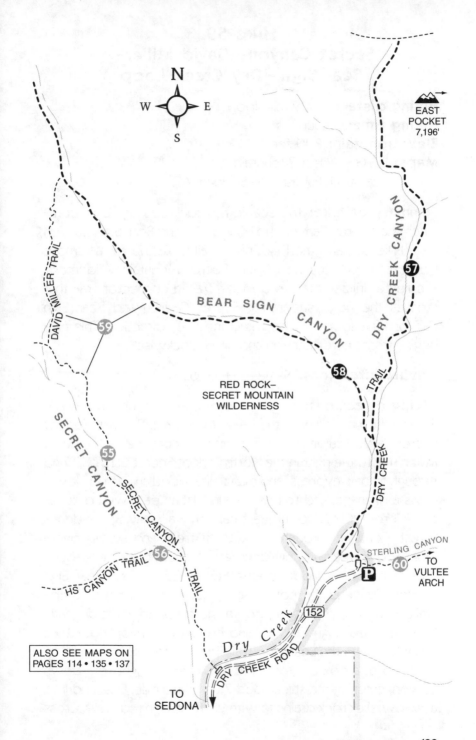

N
W · E
S

EAST
POCKET
7,196'

DAVID MILLER TRAIL

BEAR SIGN CANYON

DRY CREEK CANYON

57

58

59

TRAIL

RED ROCK–
SECRET MOUNTAIN
WILDERNESS

SECRET CANYON

55

SECRET CANYON

56

HS CANYON TRAIL

TRAIL

DRY CREEK

STERLING CANYON

60

TO
VULTEE
ARCH

P

152

Dry Creek

DRY CREEK ROAD

TO
SEDONA

ALSO SEE MAPS ON
PAGES 114 • 135 • 137

Hike 59
Secret Canyon—David Miller—
Bear Sign—Dry Creek Loop

Hiking distance: 6.2 mile loop
Hiking time: 3 hours
Elevation gain: 800 feet
Maps: U.S.G.S. Wilson Mountain
Beartooth Publishing—Sedona, AZ

Summary of hike: This scenic red rock country loop combines the Secret Canyon Trail (Hike 55), the Bear Sign Canyon Trail (Hike 58), and the Dry Creek Trail (Hike 57) for a remote journey through the Red Rock—Secret Mountain Wilderness. The route utilizes the David Miller Trail, a connector trail that crosses the ridge separating Secret Canyon and Bear Sign Canyon. The loop can be hiked in either direction. This hike begins from Secret Canyon and hikes clockwise.

Driving directions: Same as Hike 55.

Hiking directions: Follow the Secret Canyon Trail—Hike 55—to the junction with the David Miller Trail. The main fork of Secret Canyon curves west. For this hike, continue on the David Miller Trail to the right in the North Fork of Secret Canyon. Wind through an oak, cypress, and manzanita woodland. Drop down, cross a drainage, and follow the undulating path with patches of slick rock. Climb up the east canyon wall, leaving the dense forest. Continue through pockets of trees and across overlooks with sweeping 360-degree vistas. Climb a steep, rocky quarter mile to a saddle above Secret Canyon and Bear Sign Canyon. Descend the north-facing slope in a narrow, steep-walled canyon, zigzagging down the forested, cliffside path. Drop into Bear Sign Canyon, and cross the canyon floor to a T-junction with the Bear Sign Trail. The left fork heads a mile to the head of a box canyon (Hike 58). Take the right fork down canyon, crossing the streambed 7 times in a mile. Descend into a narrow, slick rock drainage with 25-foot-high red walls. Cross the stream 6 more times to the confluence of the Bear Sign and Dry Creek drainages. Cross to the east side of the creek, and continue to the right on the Dry Creek Trail. Cross the creek two more times to the trailhead at the end of Dry Creek Road/ FS Road 152. Return 0.9 miles down the road to the right.

SECRET CANYON–DAVID MILLER–
BEAR SIGN–DRY CREEK LOOP

Hike 60
Vultee Arch Trail

Hiking distance: 3.5 miles round trip
Hiking time: 2 hours
Elevation gain: 400 feet
Maps: U.S.G.S. Wilson Mountain
Beartooth Publishing—Sedona, AZ

Summary of hike: Vultee Arch is a 40-foot-high and 50-foot-long red sandstone arch stretching across the north wall of Sterling Canyon. The arch, which sits at the base of East Pocket Mesa, is named for Gerard Vultee, who died with his wife in 1938 when their plane crashed on the mesa. The Vultee Arch Trail follows Sterling Canyon in the gorgeous red rock country through groves of Arizona cypress, ponderosa pine, manzanita, scrub oak, and juniper. A short side path ends on a sandstone bench, with north views toward the stone bridge. Vultee Arch is surrounded by Lost Wilson Mountain, Secret Mountain, and East Pocket in the Red Rock—Secret Mountain Wilderness. The main trail continues past Vultee Arch on the Sterling Pass Trail (Hike 9) into Oak Creek Canyon for a one-way, 4.25-mile shuttle hike.

Driving directions: Same as Hike 57.

Hiking directions: Two trails leave from the parking area. The Dry Creek Trail heads north from the back end of the parking lot. From the east side, take the posted Vultee Arch Trail. Head east, entering the mouth of Sterling Canyon and the Red Rock—Secret Mountain Wilderness. Stroll along the canyon floor under the towering vertical face of Lost Wilson Mountain to the south. At 1.6 miles is a posted junction. The right fork climbs to Sterling Pass and descends into Oak Creek Canyon (Hike 9). Take the Vultee Arch Trail 70 yards to the left to the Vultee Arch viewpoint on a large red rock slab. From this outcrop, the arch is in full view a quarter mile across the box canyon on the north wall. This is our turn-around spot.

To hike farther, the trail continue 2.5 miles east, climbing over Sterling Pass and descending into Oak Creek Canyon (Hike 9).

⑦ SLIDE ROCK STATE PARK

SHUTTLE CAR Ⓟ

89A

OAK CREEK CANYON

⑧

STERLING PASS

⑨

STERLING PASS TRAIL

VULTEE ARCH •

N E S W

EAST POCKET 7,196'

LOST WILSON MOUNTAIN 6,762'

DRY CREEK CANYON

DRY CREEK

STERLING CANYON

⑤⑦

TRAIL

RED ROCK– SECRET MOUNTAIN WILDERNESS

⑤⑧

BEAR SIGN CANYON

Dry

SECRET MTN 6,616'

Ⓟ

ALSO SEE MAPS ON PAGES 31 • 114 • 133

152

Creek

DRY CREEK ROAD (VULTEE ARCH RD)

VULTEE ARCH TRAIL

▼ TO SEDONA

Hike 61
Sedona Centennial Trail

Hiking distance: 1 mile round trip
Hiking time: 30 minutes
Elevation gain: 200 feet
Maps: U.S.G.S. Sedona

Summary of hike: The Sedona Centennial Trail is a short, easy trail through a pinyon pine forest to an overlook. The trailhead is located at the north end of Sedona Cultural Park by the Girdner Trail (Hike 62). The wide trail leads to a scenic vista with views across the basin to the Red Rock Country, including Mingus Mountain, Cockscomb, Doe Mountain, Bear Mountain, and Secret Mountain.

Driving directions: From the Sedona Y (Highways 89A and 179 junction), drive 4.2 miles southwest on Highway 89A (towards Cottonwood) to Cultural Park Place. Turn right and drive 0.2 miles to the posted Upper Parking East on the right.

Hiking directions: From the trailhead, the signed Girdner Trail (Hike 62) heads straight ahead (north). Take the posted Sedona Centennial Trail to the right, and loop around the edge of the draw. Drop down to the lower level and a trail fork, with vistas across the Dry Creek Basin. The signed Girdner Trail continues to the right (north). Cross the trail, staying on the Sedona Centennial Trail through scattered pinyon pines and junipers to an unpaved road (Cultural Park Place). Cross the road and continue through the open forest to a fork with the View Loop Trail. Begin the short 0.1-mile loop to the right. The views extend to the east of Munds Mountain, Schnebly Hill, and Mitten Ridge; to the northeast of Wilson Mountain, Sugarloaf, Chimney Rock, and Capitol Butte; and northward across the basin to Secret Mountain. Complete the loop and return along the same path.

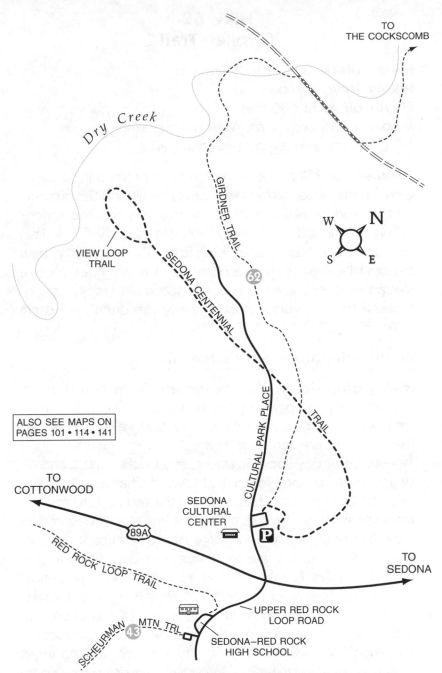

TO
THE COCKSCOMB

Dry Creek

GIRDNER TRAIL

VIEW LOOP
TRAIL

SEDONA CENTENNIAL

62

W N
S E

CULTURAL PARK PLACE

TRAIL

ALSO SEE MAPS ON
PAGES 101 • 114 • 141

TO
COTTONWOOD

SEDONA
CULTURAL
CENTER

89A

P

RED ROCK LOOP TRAIL

TO
SEDONA

UPPER RED ROCK
LOOP ROAD

SCHEURMAN MTN. TRL.
43

SEDONA–RED ROCK
HIGH SCHOOL

SEDONA CENTENNIAL TRAIL

Hike 62
Girdner Trail

Hiking distance: 9 miles round trip
Hiking time: 4.5 hours
Elevation gain: 600 feet
Maps: U.S.G.S. Sedona and Wilson Mountain
       Beartooth Publishing—Sedona, AZ

Summary of hike: The Girdner Trail was named in honor of Glen Girdner, a mail carrier between Cornville and Sedona during the years of 1918 and 1922. The trail connects the Sedona Cultural Center off of Highway 89A with the Dry Creek Basin near Dry Creek Road/Vultee Arch Road. The meandering path crosses hills, small canyons, and Dry Creek as it winds through a shaded woodland in a red rock landscape with rocky gorges. It intersects a network of trails in the Cockscomb Trail System (Hikes 63 and 64).

Driving directions: Same as Hike 61.

Hiking directions: Take the signed Girdner Trail north through scattered pinyon pines and junipers. Drop down to the lower level and a trail fork with the Sedona Centennial Trail (Hike 61). Vistas extend across the Dry Creek Basin to Wilson Mountain, Chimney Rock, Sugarloaf, and Cockscomb. Continue straight ahead on the Girdner Trail towards the basin through a beautiful open forest surrounded by the red rock formations rimming the valley. Traverse the hillside and slowly descend to the valley floor, reaching the edge of the Dry Creek drainage at one mile. Cross the drainage twice, and join a utility access road at 1.5 miles. Follow the road a short distance, and rejoin the Girdner Trail, heading north. Follow the Dry Creek drainage, crossing it a few more times to a posted T-junction with the Rupp Trail. The left fork heads uphill to the Cockscomb formation (Hike 63). Bear right on the Girdner Trail and cross Dry Creek. Head up the rocky jeep road, crossing over a ridge, and descend to a junction with the Arizona Cypress Trail on the left. Stay to the right and cross a draw to a posted junction with the Two Fences Trail on the right, surrounded by rolling hills. Stay on the Girdner Trail to the left, and curve through the rolling hills, steadily gaining elevation. At the top of the rise, head east towards Capitol Butte and Chimney Rock. As you approach Dry Creek Road, curve right, parallel to the road, to the trail's end by Vultee Arch Road (F.S. Road 152).

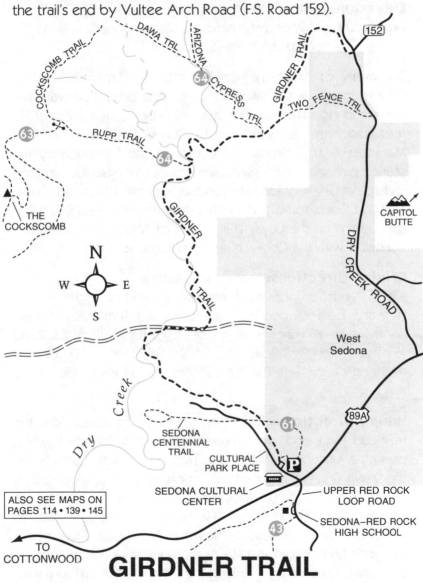

GIRDNER TRAIL

Hike 63
The Cockscomb Summit
COCKSCOMB AREA TRAILS

Hiking distance: 4.8 miles round trip
Hiking time: 2.5 hours
Elevation gain: 500 feet
Maps: U.S.G.S. Wilson Mountain and Sedona
Beartooth Publishing—Sedona, AZ

map next page

Summary of hike: The Cockscomb is a magnificent red rock formation with scalloped spires that extend skyward like the comb of a rooster. The dramatic rock sculpture sits 600 feet above the valley floor in Dry Creek Basin, south of Doe Mountain. A trail climbs to the top of the formation by the scarlet pinnacles, with sweeping vistas amongst the fantastic red rocks. The Cockscomb can be accessed from the Dawa Trail and Cockscomb Trail, both off of Boynton Pass Road. This hike begins on the Dawa Trail, south of Mescal Mountain, and connects with the Cockscomb Trail en route.

Driving directions: From the Sedona Y (Highways 89A and 179 junction), drive 3.1 miles southwest on Highway 89A (towards Cottonwood) to Dry Creek Road. Turn right and drive 2.9 miles to a T-junction at a stop sign. Turn left on F.S. Road 152C (Boynton Pass Road), and drive 0.5 miles to the posted trailhead on the left. Parking pullouts are on each side of the road.

Hiking directions: Take the closed jeep road past the trailhead map, and wind through the open forested valley, passing a junction with the O.K. Trail on the left. Continue on the Dawa Trail in the general direction of the flat-topped Doe Mountain (westward). Cross the rolling terrain to a T-junction with the Cockscomb Trail at 0.9 miles. The right fork leads to the Cockscomb Trailhead on Boynton Pass Road. Bear left for 30 yards on the combined Cockscomb–Dawa Trail, where the trails split. Take the right fork on the Cockscomb Trail up a small rise with southern views. Descend along the south face of Doe Mountain towards the east flank of Cockscomb. Continue to an old barbed-wire fence and a junction where the Cockscomb Trail ends and the Rupp Trail begins. Leave the designated trail and bear right, passing through the gated fence. Follow the fenceline towards the east base of the Cockscomb formation. Ascend the foothills to a "Public Trail" sign at a gated ranch entrance on the right. Just past the sign, the main trail curves left and follows the base of the mountain. On the curve, veer right on the cairn-marked footpath. Zigzag up the formation's northeast corner, following the cairns. Below the summit, head south along the cliff edge. Curve to the south face and climb steep rock steps to the other-worldly formations at the summit. Explore the chiseled red rocks along the small multi-fingered summit. Return by retracing your steps.

Hike 64
Dawa—Cockscomb—Rupp—
Girdner—Arizona Cypress Loop
COCKSCOMB AREA TRAILS

Hiking distance: 5 mile loop
Hiking time: 2.5 hours
Elevation gain: 200 feet
Maps: U.S.G.S. Wilson Mountain and Sedona
      Beartooth Publishing—Sedona, AZ

map next page

Summary of hike: The Cockscomb Area Trails are a network of trails that crisscross the Dry Creek Basin on footpaths and closed jeep roads at the north edge of Sedona. The trails weave through the red rock landscape across rolling hills, rocky gorges, streambeds, and seasonal creeks in a pinyon pine, juniper, and oak woodland. Five trailheads access the Cockscomb Area Trails, offering various loops and one-way shuttle hikes. This hike begins on the Dawa Trail and forms a 5-trail loop along the east side of Doe Mountain and The Cockscomb.

Driving directions: Same as Hike 63.

Hiking directions: Take the closed jeep road past the trailhead map, and stroll through the open forested valley 100 yards to a posted junction with the O.K. Trail on the left. Begin the loop to the right on the Dawa Trail, heading in the general direction of Doe Mountain (westward). Cross the rolling terrain to a T-junction with the Cockscomb Trail at 0.9 miles. The right fork leads to the Cockscomb Trailhead on Boynton Pass Road. Bear left for 30 yards on the combined Cockscomb–Dawa Trail, where the trails split. Take the right fork on the Cockscomb Trail. Descend along the south face of Doe Mountain towards The Cockscomb. Continue to an old barbed-wire fence and a junction where the Cockscomb Trail ends and the Rupp Trail begins. The trail up The Cockscomb (Hike 63) leaves the main designated trail and bears right through the gated fence. Continue straight on the Rupp Trail, curving east toward Capitol Butte. Descend to the end of the Rupp Trail at a junction with the Girdner Trail. The right fork leads to the Sedona Cultural Center off of Highway 89A (Hike 62). Continue straight on the left fork of the Girdner Trail and cross Dry Creek. Head up the rocky jeep road, crossing over a ridge, and descend to a junction with the Arizona Cypress Trail on the left. The Girdner Trail continues straight ahead towards Capitol Butte. Bear left and traverse the rolling hills, crossing Dry Creek two more times to the signed Dawa Trail on the left. Continue straight, parallel to the east bank of the creek. Make a final crossing at a posted junction. Curve left on the O.K. Trail, completing the loop at the Dawa Trail. Return to the trailhead 100 yards to the right.

HIKE 63
THE COCKSCOMB SUMMIT
HIKE 64
DAWA–COCKSCOMB–RUPP–GIRDNER– ARIZONA CYPRESS LOOP
COCKSCOMB AREA TRAILS

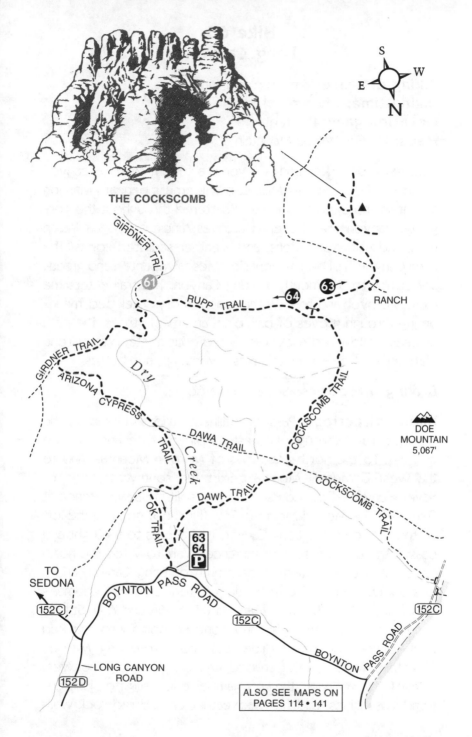

THE COCKSCOMB

GIRDNER TRL

61

RUPP TRAIL

64   63

RANCH

GIRDNER TRAIL

ARIZONA

CYPRESS

TRAIL

D r y

Creek

DAWA TRAIL

COCKSCOMB TRAIL

DOE
MOUNTAIN
5,067'

COCKSCOMB TRAIL

OK TRAIL

DAWA TRAIL

63
64
P

TO
SEDONA

152C

BOYNTON PASS ROAD

152C

152C

BOYNTON PASS ROAD

LONG CANYON
ROAD

152D

ALSO SEE MAPS ON
PAGES 114 • 141

S
E   W
N

Hike 65
Long Canyon

Hiking distance: 6 miles round trip
Hiking time: 3 hours
Elevation gain: 450 feet
Maps: U.S.G.S. Wilson Mountain

Summary of hike: Long Canyon is a stream-fed box canyon in the Red Rock–Secret Mountain Wilderness beneath Maroon Mountain and Secret Mountain. Scattered throughout the gorgeous canyon are sheltered alcoves, ancient Sinagua Indian ruins, red rock formations, and weather-sculpted spires. The Long Canyon Trail begins alongside Mescal Mountain and gradually climbs to the mouth of Long Canyon. The trail enters the narrow canyon and follows the generally dry creek bed, meandering through groves of oak, pine, and maple trees. The path crosses shallow red rock washes and ends at steep sandstone bluffs in a cul-de-sac with caves, overhangs, and buttes.

Driving directions: Same as Hike 66.

Hiking directions: Pass the trailhead map and head up the old jeep road through a forest of pinyon pine and Arizona cypress. To the north are views of Maroon Mountain and to the west is Mescal Mountain. Skirt the southwest edge of Seven Canyons Golf Course to a trail split by a wire fence at 0.6 miles. The Mescal Mountain Trail (Hike 66) goes to the left on the old road. The Long Canyon Trail curves to the right and passes through the fenced entrance. Walk towards the north tip of Mescal Mountain at the mouth of Long Canyon and a posted junction at one mile. The left fork crosses Deadman's Pass (Hike 67) to Boynton Canyon (Hikes 68 and 69). Stay in Long Canyon to the right, and continue north into the Red Rock–Secret Mountain Wilderness under towering Maroon Mountain. Wind up the shaded canyon floor on the west side of the drainage through gambel oaks, alligator junipers, ponderosa pines, and fir. The weather-carved red rock walls narrow, with scenic buttes, pillars, spires, secluded coves, and caves lining the canyon. Follow the ups and downs of the rolling terrain, crossing the creekbed numerous times. Climb up the edge of the drainage to an overhanging red rock cave and a trail split. The right fork traverses the cliff east into a narrow side canyon. Take the left fork along the overhang to a second cave. The trail soon ends at the head of the box canyon, with a great view down the length of Long Canyon.

MAROON
MOUNTAIN
6,666'

MUSHROOM
ROCK
5,848'

LONG CANYON

LONG CANYON TRAIL

N
W — E
S

RED ROCK–
SECRET MOUNTAIN
WILDERNESS

BOYNTON CANYON TRAIL

BOYNTON
SPIRES

69

68

DEADMAN'S PASS TRAIL

67

66

MESCAL MTN
TRAIL

SEVEN
CANYONS

152D

GRASSY KNOLLS

CANYON ROAD

ENCHANTMENT
RESORT

ALSO SEE MAPS ON
PAGES 114 • 149 • 151

P

LONG
CANYON

BOYNTON PASS ROAD

152C

LONG Dry Creek

TO
SEDONA

Hike 66
Mescal Mountain

Hiking distance: 6 miles round trip
Hiking time: 3 hours
Elevation gain: 450 feet
Maps: U.S.G.S. Wilson Mountain

Summary of hike: Mescal Mountain is an odd-shaped, three-fingered mountain at the mouth of Boynton Canyon and Long Canyon. The hike up Mescal Mountain ascends the east face of the mountain to ancient Indian ruins and the mesa. From the small plateau atop the mountain are sweeping vistas of the isolated ridges, buttes, and mesas between Secret Canyon, Long Canyon, and Boynton Canyon.

Driving directions: From the Sedona Y (Highways 89A and 179 junction), drive 3.1 miles southwest on Highway 89A (towards Cottonwood) to Dry Creek Road. Turn right and drive 2.9 miles to a T-junction at a stop sign. Turn right on Long Canyon Road (F.S. Road 152D), and drive 0.6 miles to the posted Long Canyon parking pullout on the left.

Hiking directions: Pass the trailhead map and head up the wide path through a forest of pinyon pine and Arizona cypress. To the north are views of Maroon Mountain and to the west is Mescal Mountain. Skirt the southwest edge of Seven Canyons Golf Course to a trail split by a wire fence at 0.6 miles. The Long Canyon Trail (Hike 65) curves right, passing through the fence. The trail to Mescal Mountain stays to the left. Curve west on the old road toward the prominent mountain. Walk towards the saddle between the main body of Mescal Mountain and its north finger. Near the base of the towering red rock formation, the trail narrows from a road to a footpath. Caves can be spotted in the east-facing cliffs. Zigzag up the cliffs towards the saddle. A cairn-marked side path on the right detours to an overlook at a cave. The rocky main trail climbs to a red rock ledge just below the saddle. Walk along the ledge to a fragile

Indian ruin in a cave. From this ledge are spectacular views across the forested valley to the surrounding mountains. Natural rock steps lead to the narrow saddle overlooking Deadman's Pass, Boynton Spires, Maroon Mountain, and Secret Mountain. Follow the saddle 20 yards south to a circular rock-lined fire pit and dwelling ruins. A level path follows the ridge west to an overlook. The main trail continues south to the vertical cliffs at the base of the upper mountain. Reaching the upper summit involves some serious rock climbing. Return north and make the easy climb to the summit of the protruding north finger with 360-degree panoramas. After savoring the views, return the same way.

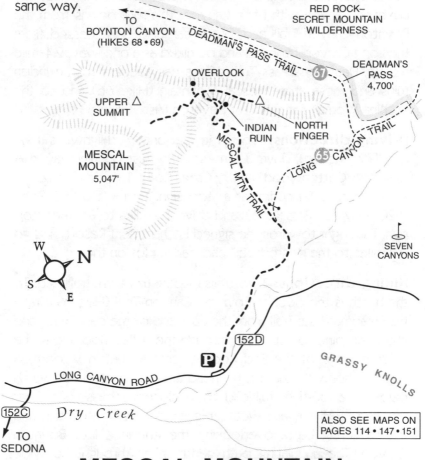

MESCAL MOUNTAIN

Hike 67
Deadman's Pass Trail

Hiking distance: 2.8 miles round trip
Hiking time: 1.5 hours
Elevation gain: 175 feet
Maps: U.S.G.S. Wilson Mountain

Summary of hike: Deadman's Pass is a low, sloping pass in a scenic corridor between Mescal Mountain and the majestic terra cotta buttes and pillars of Boynton Canyon. The Deadman's Pass Trail is a connector trail, linking the mouth of Boynton Canyon with Long Canyon. This hike begins from the Boynton Canyon Trailhead, but it can also be accessed from the Long Canyon Trailhead and be hiked as a one-way, 2.4-mile shuttle. Deadman's Pass Trail offers easy access to the Indian ruins and mesa atop Mescal Mountain (Hike 66) and to the Kachina Woman formation at Boynton Vista (Hike 68).

Driving directions: From the Sedona Y (Highways 89A and 179 junction), drive 3.1 miles southwest on Highway 89A (towards Cottonwood) to Dry Creek Road. Turn right and drive 2.9 miles to a T-junction at a stop sign. Turn left on F.S. Road 152C (Boynton Pass Road), and drive 1.6 miles to another stop sign. Turn right towards the signed Enchantment Resort, and go 0.2 miles to the posted trailhead parking lot on the right.

Hiking directions: Two trails depart from this trailhead. To the north is the popular Boynton Canyon Trail (Hike 69). Take the Deadman Pass Trail from the east end of the parking lot and enter the pine forest. Wind through the valley floor along the outside edge of the Red Rock–Secret Mountain Wilderness to a junction with the old trailhead access, located 300 yards below the existing trailhead by a closed access road. Bear left and head toward weather-carved Mescal Mountain and the towering butte overlooking the entrance into Boynton Canyon. The undulating path gently rises through the wide canyon, parallel to utility poles and between red rock cliffs and eroded formations. Pass a natural amphitheater and cross the low 4,700-foot Deadman's Pass at the north tip of Mescal Mountain. Gradually descend, with great views of Seven Canyons Golf Course, Long Canyon, Maroon Mountain, and Wilson Mountain. At 1.4 miles, curve right to a signed junction with the Long Canyon Trail. This is the turn-around spot.

To hike farther, the right fork leads to Mescal Mountain (Hike 66) and one mile to the Long Canyon trailhead. The left fork continues into Long Canyon (Hike 65).

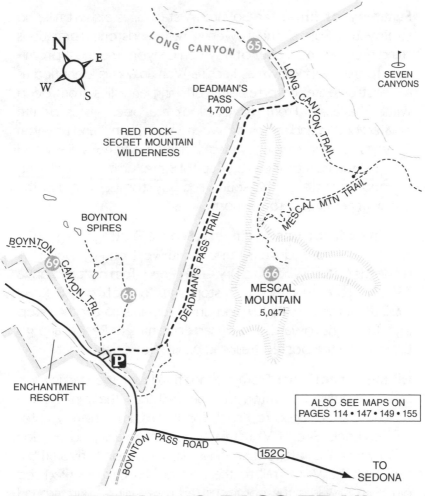

DEADMAN'S PASS TRAIL

Hike 68
Boynton Vista Trail
BOYNTON SPIRES · KACHINA WOMAN

Hiking distance: 0.7 miles round trip
Hiking time: 30 minutes
Elevation gain: 300 feet
Maps: U.S.G.S. Wilson Mountain
  Beartooth Publishing—Sedona, AZ

Summary of hike: The Boynton Vista Trail is a short hike up to Boynton Spires. The towering red sandstone formations stand guard at the mouth of Boynton Canyon. The most prominent formation is known as Kachina Woman and is identified as an electromagnetic vortex site, drawing energies from deep within the earth. From the overlook are open vistas of the isolated buttes and mesas between Secret, Long, and Boynton Canyons. The sweeping views include Deadman's Pass and Mescal Mountain to the east; Capitol Butte, Chimney Rock, and Courthouse Butte to the south; and Boynton Canyon and the Enchantment Resort to the north.

Driving directions: From the Sedona Y (Highways 89A and 179 junction), drive 3.1 miles southwest on Highway 89A (towards Cottonwood) to Dry Creek Road. Turn right and drive 2.9 miles to a T-junction at a stop sign. Turn left on F.S. Road 152C (Boynton Pass Road), and drive 1.6 miles to another stop sign. Turn right towards the signed Enchantment Resort and go 0.2 miles to the posted trailhead parking lot on the right.

Hiking directions: From the north side of the parking lot, take the posted Boynton Canyon Trail into the pine forest beneath the sculpted red rock formations. Immediately enter the Red Rock—Secret Mountain Wilderness to a signed junction at 50 yards. The left fork continues into Boynton Canyon (Hike 69). Take the Vista Trail to the right on the cairn-marked red dirt path towards the gorgeous red rock spires. Skirt around to the east side of the spires and ascend the summit, heading west to the saddle between the sculpted formations. After savoring the views and spiritual energies, return by retracing your steps.

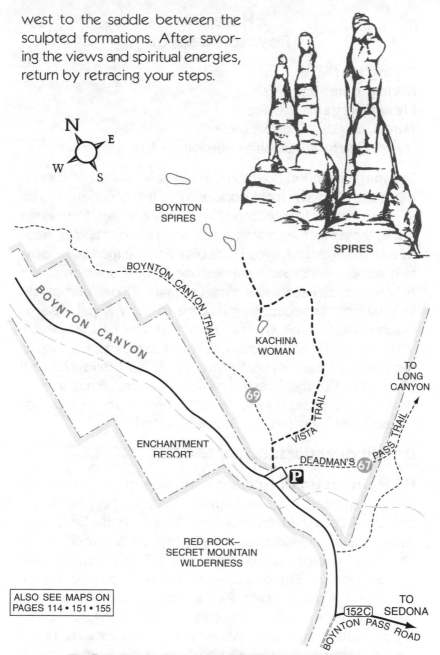

N
E
W
S

BOYNTON SPIRES

SPIRES

BOYNTON CANYON TRAIL

BOYNTON CANYON

KACHINA WOMAN

TO LONG CANYON

69

VISTA TRAIL

PASS TRAIL

ENCHANTMENT RESORT

DEADMAN'S 67

P

RED ROCK– SECRET MOUNTAIN WILDERNESS

ALSO SEE MAPS ON PAGES 114 • 151 • 155

TO SEDONA

152C

BOYNTON PASS ROAD

BOYNTON VISTA TRAIL
BOYNTON SPIRES • KACHINA WOMAN

Hike 69
Boynton Canyon

Hiking distance: 5 miles round trip
Hiking time: 2.5 hours
Elevation gain: 500 feet
Maps: U.S.G.S. Wilson Mountain
Beartooth Publishing—Sedona, AZ

Summary of hike: Boynton Canyon is an awesome canyon and one of Sedona's most popular areas. It is considered to be an electromagnetic vortex site, drawing energies from deep within the earth. The canyon is rich with red rock buttes, hoodoo rock spires, and jagged red formations on the 1,000-foot-high vertical sandstone and limestone cliffs. In addition to the truly spectacular scenery are ancient Sinagua Indian cliff dwellings, which retain special significance to the Yavapai/Apache Indians. The trail follows the sheer east wall of the canyon, skirting the edge of Enchantment Resort, which sprawls across the mouth of the canyon. Beyond the luxury resort, the path drops down to the forested canyon floor and winds through ponderosa pine and Douglas fir to the back of the box canyon beneath Bear Mountain and Secret Mountain.

Driving directions: Same as Hike 68.

Hiking directions: From the north side of the parking lot, take the posted Boynton Canyon Trail into the pine forest beneath the sculpted red rock formations. Enter the Red Rock–Secret Mountain Wilderness to a signed junction at 50 yards. The Vista Trail climbs up to an overlook at Boynton Spires (Hike 68). Stay on the Boynton Canyon Trail, and continue straight ahead on the red dirt path. Pass a vertical rock wall, and traverse the contours of the east canyon wall, skirting the boundary of Enchantment Resort. At one mile, as you leave the resort behind, descend to the canyon floor. (The Forest Service closed off the footpath on the right, which scrambled up the hillside to prehistoric Indian ruins in an alcove of red rock.) Cross the streambed and wind along the canyon bottom through alligator-bark junipers, oaks, and pines. Gradually gain elevation through tall native brush between the stunning red-walled canyon with caves and spires. At 1.5 miles, the canyon curves west and the vertical walls narrow. Cross the streambed to the north wall as the grade steepens. The trail ends near the end of the box canyon at a Forest Service sign and an overlook on a slope between Secret Mountain and Bear Mountain.

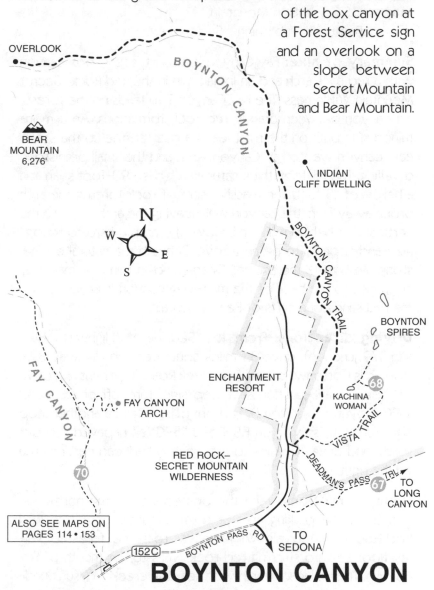

OVERLOOK

BOYNTON CANYON

BEAR MOUNTAIN 6,276'

INDIAN CLIFF DWELLING

N
W
E
S

BOYNTON CANYON TRAIL

BOYNTON SPIRES

ENCHANTMENT RESORT

FAY CANYON

FAY CANYON ARCH

KACHINA WOMAN

68

VISTA TRAIL

RED ROCK–SECRET MOUNTAIN WILDERNESS

70

DEADMAN'S PASS TRL

67

TO LONG CANYON

ALSO SEE MAPS ON PAGES 114 • 153

152C

BOYNTON PASS RD

TO SEDONA

BOYNTON CANYON

Hike 70
Fay Canyon Trail

Hiking distance: 2.4 miles round trip
Hiking time: 1.5 hours
Elevation gain: 300 feet
Maps: U.S.G.S. Wilson Mountain
      Beartooth Publishing—Sedona, AZ

Summary of hike: Fay Canyon is a short, scenic box canyon with a red rock arch and an Indian ruin in the Red Rock—Secret Mountain Wilderness. The Fay Canyon Trail leads up the forested canyon between craggy red rock formations. An unmaintained side path on the right leads a quarter mile up the steep east canyon wall to Fay Canyon Arch and the small prehistoric dwelling. The 25-foot-thick natural arch has a 90-foot span and a height of 15 feet. The massive slab of rock forming the arch broke away from the canyon wall, leaving the arch close to the vertical cliff behind it. From below, the arch is hard to recognize and appears to be an alcove. Beneath the natural bridge, stone walls mark the ancient Sinagua Indian ruin. The main trail continues to the back of the mile-long canyon, surrounded by the red sandstone cliffs of Bear Mountain.

Driving directions: From the Sedona Y (Highways 89A and 179 junction), drive 3.1 miles southwest on Highway 89A (towards Cottonwood) to Dry Creek Road. Turn right and drive 2.9 miles to a T-junction at a stop sign. Turn left on F.S. Road 152C (Boynton Pass Road), and drive 1.6 miles to another stop sign. Turn left, staying on F.S. Road 152C (an unpaved red dirt road), and drive 0.5 miles to the posted trailhead parking area on the right.

Hiking directions: Take the posted trail at the northwest corner of the parking area, and immediately enter the Red Rock—Secret Mountain Wilderness. Cross the forested valley floor toward stunning red rock walls to the mouth of Fay Canyon. The trail leads northwest near the creekbed, surrounded by the cliffs of Bear Mountain. At a half mile, an unmaintained, cairn-marked path leaves the main trail to the right. Detour on this footpath and cross the creekbed toward the west-facing cliffs. Scramble a quarter mile up the cliffs, gaining 100 feet up to the base of the arch. The footwork is tricky and caution is advised. Hike under and behind the arch for a framed view of Bear Mountain. After exploring the ancient ruin, return to the main trail and continue up canyon. The trail ends at a fork in the canyon by a large rock slide. Paths curve a short distance in both directions into the narrow box canyons, reaching rock shelves surrounded by steep cliffs and sky-ward views rising above the forest.

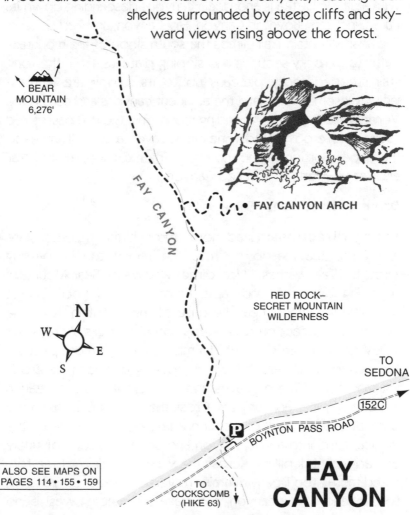

BEAR
MOUNTAIN
6,276'

FAY CANYON

FAY CANYON ARCH

RED ROCK–
SECRET MOUNTAIN
WILDERNESS

N
W   E
S

TO
SEDONA

152C

P

BOYNTON PASS ROAD

ALSO SEE MAPS ON
PAGES 114 • 155 • 159

TO
COCKSCOMB
(HIKE 63)

FAY
CANYON

Hike 71
Bear Mountain Trail

Hiking distance: 4.8 miles round trip
Hiking time: 3 hours
Elevation gain: 1,700 feet
Maps: U.S.G.S. Wilson Mountain and Loy Butte
      Beartooth Publishing—Sedona, AZ

Summary of hike: Bear Mountain is a prominent mountain with multiple plateaus and deep canyons descending down its flanks, including Boynton Canyon, Fay Canyon, and Red Canyon. The Bear Mountain Trail climbs the south slope of the mountain, with steep rocky sections and sloping plateaus. From the four, stair-stepped rocky plateaus up to its summit are increasingly awesome views into the adjacent canyons and across the Verde Valley to the surrounding mountains. The trail passes red rock pillars, eroding sandstone cliffs, caves, and small arches to the upper portion of the mountain. The exposed, rugged trail ends at an overlook into Red Canyon.

Driving directions: Same as Hike 72.

Hiking directions: Head north through the trailhead gate and enter the meadow. Cross the rolling terrain, passing through three washes. Head directly towards Bear Mountain, towering over the landscape. Enter the Red Rock—Secret Mountain Wilderness near the base of the mountain. Begin the northbound ascent on rock steps and slab rocks. Across the valley floor are eroded cuts forming a massive mosaic across the meadowland. Pass through an opening between the eroding sandstone cliffs by caves and small arches to a plateau in a grove of pines and junipers. Cross the sloping plateau to the base of the red rock pillars. Curve left along the base of the vertical cliffs into a side canyon and another garden of finely etched red rock pillars. Across the valley is a view of the forested mesa atop Doe Mountain. Traverse the east canyon wall to the head of the canyon, and make a sweeping west bend across the towering bowl. Climb out of the bowl on rock slab steps to another plateau, which appears to be the summit but is not. Head north on the sloping, chaparral-covered plateau to an overlook of Fay Canyon. Curve left to the end of the trail, perched on the cliffs overlooking Red Canyon. Return on the same path.

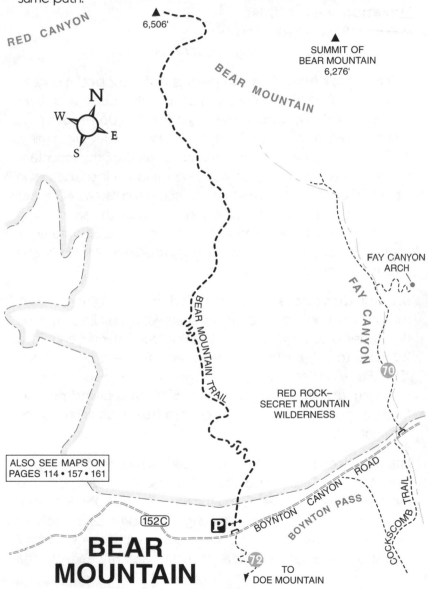

ALSO SEE MAPS ON
PAGES 114 • 157 • 161

Hike 72
Doe Mountain Trail

Hiking distance: 1.5 miles round trip to summit
Add 1.25 miles to loop the mesa perimeter
Hiking time: 1—2 hours
Elevation gain: 400 feet
Maps: U.S.G.S. Wilson Mountain
Beartooth Publishing—Sedona, AZ

Summary of hike: Doe Mountain is a flat-topped mountain in Sedona's Red Rock Country, standing alone between Bear Mountain and The Cockscomb. The small 5,067-foot mesa measures less than a half mile at its widest point. A zigzagging, well-maintained path ascends the north face of the mountain, offering close-up views of the caves and rock sculptures in the weathered cliffs. From the sage-scented plateau 400 feet above the valley floor are sweeping vistas of the surrounding red rock country, including views of the entire Sedona area, Dry Creek Basin, Verde Valley, Cottonwood, the Black Hills, and Jerome, perched on the hills.

Driving directions: From the Sedona Y (Highways 89A and 179 junction), drive 3.1 miles southwest on Highway 89A (towards Cottonwood) to Dry Creek Road. Turn right and drive 2.9 miles to a T-junction at a stop sign. Turn left on F.S. Road 152C (Boynton Pass Road), and drive 1.6 miles to another stop sign. Turn left, staying on F.S. Road 152C (an unpaved red dirt road), and drive 1.3 miles to the posted trailhead parking lot on the right.

Hiking directions: Cross the road towards flat-topped Doe Mountain. Take the posted trail across the sloping basin to the base of the mountain. Climb the north face of Doe Mountain on a series of switchbacks, making the ascent easy. Steadily climb the eroded cliff face in a ravine with caves, craggy formations, and views of Bear Mountain and Fay Canyon. The maintained trail ends on the flat-topped mesa with sweeping, unobstructed vistas. Return along the same route.

To hike farther, an unmaintained 1.25-mile path loops around the perimeter of the tabletop mesa. The path meanders through low-growing chaparral with bare red rock, rock outcroppings, and never-ending views in all directions. Before circling the mesa, make a mental note of where the Doe Mountain Trail meets the rim for your return.

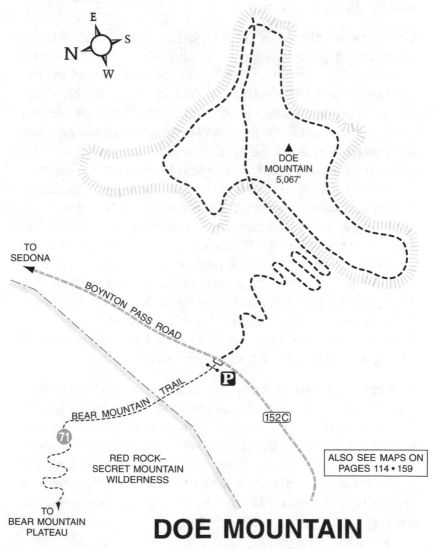

DOE MOUNTAIN

Hike 73
Palatki Ruins
Open 9:30 A.M.—4:00 P.M.

Hiking distance: Palatki Ruins: 0.5 mile loop
Rock Art Trail: 0.4 miles round trip
Hiking time: 1 hour
Elevation gain: 100 feet
Maps: U.S.G.S. Loy Butte

map
page 165

Summary of hike: The Palatki (Hopi for red house) Ruins is a protected archaeological site with 900-year-old Sinagua dwellings. The ruins sit at the mouth of Red Canyon on the western base of Bear Mountain. Within the sheltered sandstone canyon are ancient Indian pictographs (designs painted or drawn on the rock surface) and petroglyphs (drawings that are carved, scratched, pecked, pounded, or ground into the rock). The ruin was one of the largest Sinagua Indian Villages in the Sedona—Red Rock area and contains the largest concentration of prehistoric rock art in central Arizona. Two easy trails explore the red-walled canyon. The half-mile Palatki Ruins Trail leads to two separate cliff dwellings and a vista overlooking the small canyon. The 0.4-mile Rock Art Loop leads to a series of four alcoves with a rich collection of ancient art. The time period represents a long sequence of human occupation from the Archaic Period (dating back 5,000 years) through the Southern Sinagua (AD 600 to 1400), the Yavapai and Apache (AD 1300 to 1885), as well as early pioneers.

Driving directions: From the Sedona Y (Highways 89A and 179 junction), drive 9.6 miles southwest on Highway 89A (towards Cottonwood) to Red Canyon Road (Forest Service Road 525). Turn right and drive 6 miles on the unpaved road, staying on F.S. 525 to a posted Y-fork located just past the Boynton Pass Road turnoff. Veer to the right on Forest Service Road 795, and continue 1.8 miles to the posted parking area on the right.

Hiking directions: Walk up the road to the information center. Just past the center is a junction. The Ruins Trail goes to the right and the Rock Art Trail goes to the left.

RUINS TRAIL: Walk up the path to the right through an open forest to the base of the sheer vertical cliffs. Rock steps lead up to the base of the East Alcove ruins in a cirque of overhanging red rock formations. Explore the inside of the ancient two-story multi-room dwelling. The pueblos are held together with 900-year-old mortar, with juniper door and window supports. The West Alcove ruins are closed due to deterioration. Complete the loop or return to the junction by the center.

ROCK ART TRAIL: From the junction by the information center, walk towards the north canyon wall, looping behind the center. A short distance ahead is the overhanging rock cave. To the right is The Grotto, with drawings dating back as far as 5,000 years, and Sinagua animal and human art, between 900 and 1,300 years old. To the left is Bear Alcove, with Yavapai or Apache drawings of a bear and a man on a horse. The path continues to the Spring Overhang and the roasting pit at the end of the trail.

Hike 74
Loy Canyon

Hiking distance: 7.5—10 miles round trip
Hiking time: 4—5.5 hours
Elevation gain: 700—1,700 feet
Maps: U.S.G.S. Loy Butte
       Beartooth Publishing—Sedona, AZ

map
page 167

Summary of hike: Loy Canyon is a towering canyon in the Red Rock Canyons area with dramatic windswept formations and Indian dwellings on the overhanging cliffs. Samuel Loy and his family used the Loy Canyon Trail in the 1880s to move cattle from the Mogollon Rim to the valley. The Loy Canyon Trail follows the length of the canyon for 5 miles, gaining 1,700 feet to a junction with the Secret Mountain Trail. It is the main route to the top of Secret Mountain. The first 4 miles follows a gently sloping grade along the lush canyon floor. The last mile steeply climbs the cliffs to a saddle at the head of the canyon, connecting Secret Mountain with the Mogollon Rim.

Driving directions: From the Sedona Y (Highways 89A and 179 junction), drive 9.6 miles southwest on Highway 89A (towards Cottonwood) to Red Canyon Road (Forest Service Road 525). Turn right and drive 9.5 miles on the unpaved road to the posted trailhead on the right, just before a cattle guard and the signed entrance to Hancock Ranch. (Along the way, follow the signs to Loy Butte, staying on F.S. 525.) Park in the trailhead parking area on the left, across from the trail.

Hiking directions: Cross the road to the posted trailhead. The Loy Butte Formation sits to the north on the edge of the Red Rock–Secret Mountain Wilderness (Hike 75). Pass through a trail easement on the Hancock Ranch for a half mile, skirting the east side of the ranch along a wire fence. Drop down to the canyon bottom at the east base of Loy Butte. Cross a rocky wash, passing a ranch meadow with a red rock outbuilding. Continue past the ranch through an open forest of pine, oak, juniper, and manzanita between Secret Mountain to the east and Loy Butte to the west. Sinagua cliff dwellings can be spotted in caves and overhangs on the west canyon wall. At just over 2 miles, by a distinct 5,167-foot, bell-shaped red rock formation, the canyon forks into two drainages. Follow the right fork into the narrowing canyon with moss-covered red rocks. Curve to the right (east), beneath the towering walls of Secret Mountain and the Mogollon Rim. This is the turn-around spot for a 7.5-mile round-trip hike.

To hike farther, curve around the north base of Secret Mountain above the canyon floor. The canyon bottom soon rises and meets the trail. Walk up the forested drainage, and cross over to the north canyon wall at the base of the Mogollon Rim. Begin climbing in earnest with the aid of switchbacks, gaining 1,000 feet in the next mile. As you climb the east-facing cliffs, savor the great views into Loy Canyon. At 5 miles, the trail ends at a posted junction with the Secret Mountain Trail on a saddle connecting Secret Mountain with the Mogollon Rim. The left fork leads a quarter mile to the Secret Mountain Trailhead at the end of Forest Service Road 538. The right fork accesses the summit of Secret Mountain with an easy 200-foot climb.

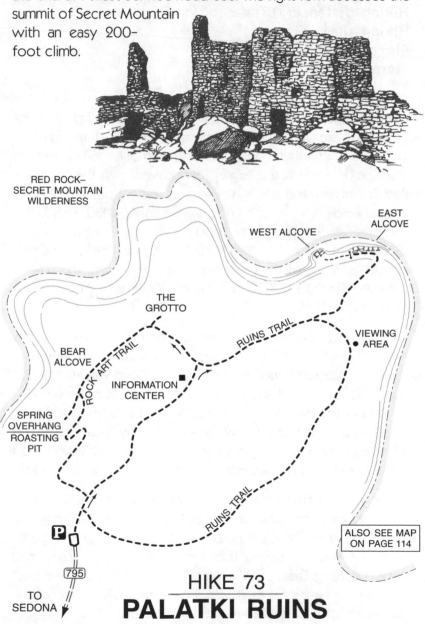

RED ROCK–
SECRET MOUNTAIN
WILDERNESS

EAST
ALCOVE

WEST ALCOVE

THE
GROTTO

RUINS TRAIL

VIEWING
● AREA

BEAR
ALCOVE

ROCK ART TRAIL

INFORMATION
CENTER

SPRING
OVERHANG
ROASTING
PIT

RUINS TRAIL

ALSO SEE MAP
ON PAGE 114

Ⓟ

795

TO
SEDONA

HIKE 73
PALATKI RUINS

Hike 75
Honanki Ruins
Open 9:30 A.M.—4:00 P.M.

Hiking distance: 0.8 miles round trip
Hiking time: 30 minutes
Elevation gain: 50 feet
Maps: U.S.G.S. Loy Butte
Beartooth Publishing—Sedona, AZ

Summary of hike: The Honanki (Hopi for bear house) Ruins sit at the base of Loy Butte on the sheltered west-facing cliffs. They are among the Red Rock Country's most significant Indian pueblos. Honanki is the largest cliff dwelling in the Sedona–Red Rocks area and among the largest ancient population sites in the Verde Valley, occupied between AD 1130—1280. The site originally contained about 60 rooms. The cave is rich with pictographs; some date back to 2000 BC, long before the cliff dwellings. Most of the pictographs are from the Sinagua and date to AD 900—1300. Others by the Yavapai or Apache date from 1400—1875.

Driving directions: From the Sedona Y (Highways 89A and 179 junction), drive 9.6 miles southwest on Highway 89A (towards Cottonwood) to Red Canyon Road (Forest Service Road 525). Turn right and drive 9.5 miles on the unpaved road to the posted Hancock Ranch entrance at the Loy Canyon trailhead. (Along the way, follow the signs to Loy Butte, staying on F.S. 525.) Continue driving through the ranch 0.7 miles (on a road easement) to the posted Honanki Ruins parking area on the left.

Hiking directions: Cross the road to the information kiosk. Pass the booth to a junction in Lincoln Canyon. Bear right, gently dropping to the base of the Loy Butte cliffs. Rock-lined paths lead to the base of the 20-foot-high pueblo walls in a huge red rock overhang. From the Western Alcove on the left, the path follows the base of the cliffs to the right, parallel to a continuous series of rock-walled rooms with pictographs.

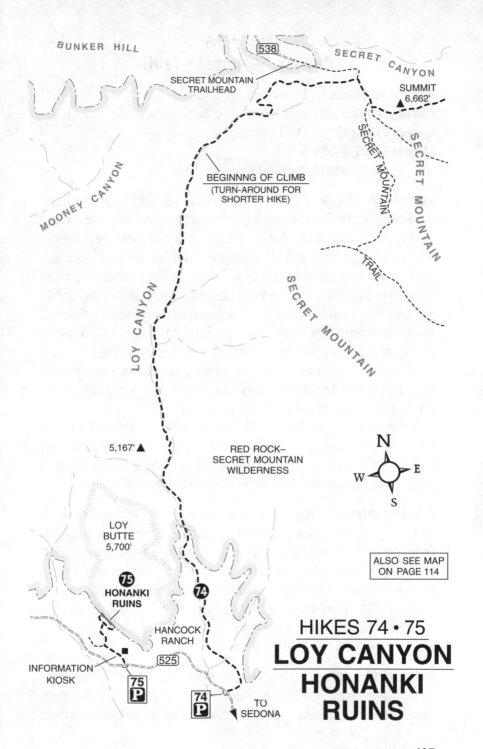

BUNKER HILL

538

SECRET CANYON

SECRET MOUNTAIN
TRAILHEAD

SUMMIT
▲ 6,662'

MOONEY CANYON

SECRET MOUNTAIN

BEGINNNG OF CLIMB
(TURN-AROUND FOR
SHORTER HIKE)

SECRET MOUNTAIN

TRAIL

LOY CANYON

SECRET MOUNTAIN

5,167' ▲

RED ROCK–
SECRET MOUNTAIN
WILDERNESS

N
W ⊕ E
S

LOY
BUTTE
5,700'

ALSO SEE MAP
ON PAGE 114

75
HONANKI
RUINS

74

HANCOCK
RANCH

INFORMATION
KIOSK

525

75
P

74
P

TO
SEDONA

HIKES 74 • 75
LOY CANYON
HONANKI
RUINS

Hike 76
Casner Mountain Trail

Hiking distance: 5 miles round trip
Hiking time: 2.5 hours
Elevation gain: 2,000 feet
Maps: U.S.G.S. Loy Butte
  Beartooth Publishing—Sedona, AZ

Summary of hike: Casner Mountain is a 6,836-foot mountain in the Red Rock Canyons area northwest of Sedona. The mountain was named after George Casner, who pastured sheep here at the turn of the 20th Century. The trail begins on an old, rocky jeep road and joins a power line access road. The road offers no shade as it climbs the south face of Casner Mountain through a narrow strip of land between the Sycamore Canyon Wilderness and the Red Rock—Secret Mountain Wilderness. Along the way, the trail zigzags up the mountain to the exposed upper slope, with views of domed Robbers Roost, Bear Mountain, Sugarloaf Mountain, and Black Mountain. From the summit are sweeping vistas of the Sycamore Canyon Wilderness Area, the Black Hills, Verde Valley, the San Francisco Peaks, a great view of Sycamore Pass, and the red rocks of Sycamore Canyon's inner gorge. The trail can be hiked as a 14-mile loop with the Mooney Trail, directly to the east.

Driving directions: From the Sedona Y (Highways 89A and 179 junction), drive 9.6 miles southwest on Highway 89A (towards Cottonwood) to Red Canyon Road (Forest Service Road 525). Turn right and drive 2.8 miles on the unpaved road to posted Forest Service Road 525C on the left. Bear left and continue 7.2 miles to a horseshoe left bend in the road. The posted trailhead is in the bend on the right. Park in the small pullouts on either side of the road.

Hiking directions: Head north from the bend in the road towards prominent Casner Mountain, looming straight ahead. Walk up the wide, rock-strewn path. Stay on the abandoned jeep road up the sloping foothills on a moderate uphill grade. At 0.4 miles, just before reaching the power poles, the trail joins the service road. Follow the power lines to the base of Casner Mountain's south face. The sweeping vistas across the basin include Loy Butte, Doe Mountain, Cockscomb, Chimney Rock, Capitol Butte, Sugarloaf, Cathedral Rock, Bear Mountain, and the rounded red rock dome of Robbers Roost. At 1.3 miles, switchbacks zigzag up Casner Mountain along the outside edge of the Red Rock–Secret Mountain Wilderness boundary. Break out onto the west slope of Casner Mountain in a half mile, with expansive views into Sycamore Canyon and the sculpted red rock towers of Sycamore Pass. Continue up the slope above the cream-colored coconino sandstone to the 6,836-foot summit. This is our turn-around spot.

To hike farther, the trail follows the power lines along the ridge, connecting with the Mooney Trail and Buck Ridge.

BUCK RIDGE

MOONEY CANYON

SYCAMORE CANYON WILDERNESS

RED ROCK–
SECRET
MOUNTAIN
WILDERNESS

MOONEY TRAIL

N
W   E
S

CASNER

CASNER   MOUNTAIN

6,836' ▲

MOUNTAIN TRAIL

SYCAMORE
PASS

DOGIE TRAIL

▲ ROBBERS
ROOST

P

ALSO SEE MAP
ON PAGE 114

CASNER
MOUNTAIN

525C

TO
▲ SEDONA

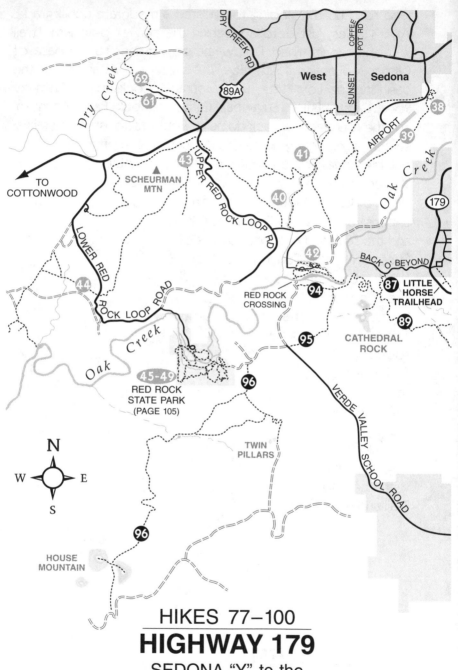

DRY CREEK RD

COFFEE POT RD

West **Sedona**

89A

SUNSET

62

61

Dry Creek

38

AIRPORT

39

TO
COTTONWOOD

SCHEURMAN
MTN

UPPER RED ROCK LOOP RD

43

41

40

Oak Creek

179

LOWER RED

42

ROCK LOOP ROAD

44

RED ROCK
CROSSING

94

BACK O' BEYOND

87 LITTLE
HORSE
TRAILHEAD

89

Oak Creek

95

CATHEDRAL
ROCK

45-49

RED ROCK
STATE PARK
(PAGE 105)

96

VERDE VALLEY SCHOOL ROAD

N
W ⊕ E
S

TWIN
PILLARS

96

HOUSE
MOUNTAIN

HIKES 77–100
HIGHWAY 179
SEDONA "Y" to the
VILLAGE of OAK CREEK

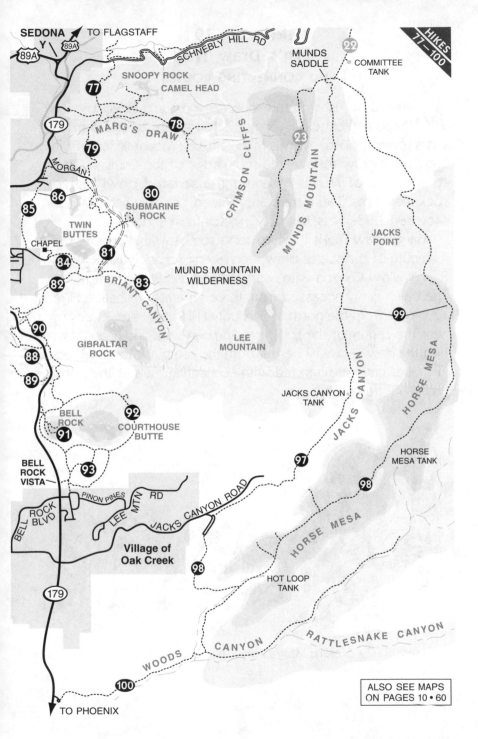

SEDONA
TO FLAGSTAFF
89A
89A
SCHNEBLY HILL RD
179
MUNDS SADDLE
22
COMMITTEE TANK
SNOOPY ROCK
CAMEL HEAD
77
MARG'S DRAW
78
CRIMSON CLIFFS
79
23
MORGAN
MUNDS MOUNTAIN
86
80
SUBMARINE ROCK
JACKS POINT
85
TWIN BUTTES
CHAPEL
81
84
MUNDS MOUNTAIN WILDERNESS
82
BRIANT CANYON
83
99
GIBRALTAR ROCK
LEE MOUNTAIN
90
HORSE MESA
88
JACKS CANYON
89
JACKS CANYON TANK
BELL ROCK
92
97
HORSE MESA TANK
91
COURTHOUSE BUTTE
98
BELL ROCK VISTA
93
HORSE MESA
PINON PINES
LEE MTN RD
JACKS CANYON ROAD
Village of Oak Creek
98
HOT LOOP TANK
BELL ROCK BLVD
179
WOODS CANYON
RATTLESNAKE CANYON
100
TO PHOENIX

ALSO SEE MAPS ON PAGES 10 • 60

Hikes 77–79
Marg's Draw Trail
AND CONNECTING ROUTES

Marg's Draw is a picturesque canyon surrounded by the fluted and chiseled geometric formations of the Crimson Cliffs (cover photo), Munds Mountain, Lee Mountain, and Twin Buttes. The draw follows the south edge of the Crimson Cliffs to the base of Munds Mountain in a serrated bowl of red rock mountains. These trails are located just inside the Munds Mountain Wilderness, but only minutes from Sedona.

Marg's Draw Trail is the main north–south trail that crosses the mouth of the scenic draw, connecting Schnebly Hill Road in Bear Wallow Canyon with Morgan Road and Battlement Mesa. The trail is easily accessed from three separate trailheads. Hike 77 begins from the north at Schnebly Hill Road. Hike 78 begins near the center of the trail from Sombart Lane and heads east into the draw. Hike 79 begins from the south at Morgan Road. The hikes can be extended with connecting trails at the north and south trailheads.

Hikes 77–79 explore Marg's Draw Trail along the Crimson Cliffs.

Hike 77
Marg's Draw Trail from Schnebly Hill Road
NORTH TRAILHEAD

Hiking distance: 2 miles round trip
Hiking time: 1 hour
Elevation gain: 100 feet
Maps: U.S.G.S. Sedona and Munds Mountain
   Beartooth Publishing—Sedona, AZ

map
page 177

Summary of hike: This hike begins from the north end of Marg's Draw Trail at the Munds Wagon trailhead on Schnebly Hill Road. The trail heads south from Bear Wallow Canyon and curves around the west slope of Camel Head and Snoopy Rock, which rise prominently at the toe of the weathered Crimson Cliffs. The path skirts the mouth of Marg's Draw, with incredible vistas of the surrounding red rock sculptures.

Driving directions: From the Sedona Y (Highways 89A and 179 junction), drive 0.3 miles south on Highway 179 (towards Phoenix) to Schnebly Hill Road and turn left. Continue 0.9 miles to the parking lot on the left, at the end of the paved section of the road.

Hiking directions: The posted trail leaves from the northwest corner of the parking lot and heads west 25 yards to a junction. The right fork detours 80 yards to a vista overlook of Steamboat Rock, Wilson Mountain, Uptown Sedona, and West Sedona. Return to the junction and continue 300 yards downhill to a Y-fork. The Huckaby Trail veers north to Midgely Bridge (Hike 17). Curve left on Marg's Draw Trail, and cross Schnebly Hill Road. Enter the Munds Mountain Wilderness, and cross a slick rock streambed. Wind through the lush forest beneath towering red rock formations. The undulating path crosses a series of rock drainages and curves around the west side of the Crimson Cliffs, with a great close-up view of Snoopy Rock. Drop over a rise, adjacent to Snoopy's feet, and descend to views of Battlement Mesa, Munds Mountain, and the sculpted south side of the Crimson Cliffs. An unsigned side path bears left and parallels the Crimson Cliffs to some of the finest red rock sculptures in Sedona (cover photo). Marg's Draw Trail continues south to a posted junction. The right fork leads 0.4 miles to a trailhead off of Sombart Lane (Hike 78). The left fork, straight ahead, continues south on Marg's Draw Trail to Morgan Road at the Broken Arrow Trailhead (Hike 79). The trail can also be hiked as a 2-mile, one-way shuttle with Hike 79.

Hike 78
Crimson Cliffs and Snoopy Rock
MARG'S DRAW

Hiking distance: 2.5 miles round trip
Hiking time: 1.5 hour
Elevation gain: 300 feet
Maps: U.S.G.S. Sedona and Munds Mountain

map
page 177

Summary of hike: This hike begins from Sombart Lane and accesses Marg's Draw Trail at the mouth of the draw. The trail is an undesignated path that follows the draw along the southern edge of the Crimson Cliffs through the valley below Munds Mountain. The Marg's Draw drainage offers a couple of distinct but unmaintained routes that are explored in this hike. The north trail winds up the Crimson Cliffs to Snoopy Rock, a profile likeness to the famous canine sleeping on his back atop the doghouse. The southern path stays on the canyon bottom and leads to large red rock mounds at the east end of the draw, in a bowl surrounded by serrated red cliffs and eroded sculptures (cover photo).

Driving directions: From the Sedona Y (Highways 89A and 179 junction), drive 0.6 miles south on Highway 179 (towards Phoenix) to Sombart Lane and turn left. Continue 0.1 miles to the posted trailhead parking lot on the left, just before the road makes a horseshoe left bend.

Hiking directions: Walk past the trailhead map board, and cross Sombart Lane at the bend in the road. Pass through the trail gate, and enter the Munds Mountain Wilderness. Climb the forested hill with natural red rock steps to the open plateau, with phenomenal views of the Crimson Cliffs and the sculpted red rock formations (cover photo). Follow the level path east to the posted T-junction with Marg's Draw Trail at 0.4 miles. The left fork heads north to Schnebly Hill Road (Hike 77). The right fork heads south to Morgan Road at the Broken Arrow Trailhead (Hike 79). Take the right fork south 40 yards to an unsigned footpath on the left. Bear left, leaving the main trail, and weave through the open forest. Parallel the south flank of the Crimson Cliffs. Work your way deeper into the weathered rock bowl, passing Snoopy Rock, from his toes to his head, and Camel Head, towering over Snoopy. The main path continues east to a huge slick rock slab in a bowl. The 360-degree vistas include Cockscomb, Chimney Rock, Casner Mountain, Battlement Mesa, Twin Buttes, Munds Mountain, and Lee Mountain. From the back (east) end of the smooth slab, trails head north and south. Take the north path, climbing up terraced red rock slabs to the back of the draw, tucked into the curvature of the Crimson Cliffs.

Return towards the head of Snoopy Rock on the same trail. Another path veers to the right to the foot of the cliffs beneath Snoopy's head. The path leads up the cliffs to the base of the spires just east of the rock formation. Explore on your own route, as multiple paths weave through the formations.

Hike 79
Marg's Draw Trail from Morgan Road
SOUTH TRAILHEAD

Hiking distance: 2 miles round trip
Hiking time: 1 hour
Elevation gain: 100 feet
Maps: U.S.G.S. Sedona and Munds Mountain
　　　　　Beartooth Publishing—Sedona, AZ

map
page 177

Summary of hike: This hike begins from the Broken Arrow Trailhead, adjacent to the base of Battlement Mesa. The trail heads north and parallels Munds Mountain through an open expanse dotted with Arizona cypress, pinyon pines, and junipers. The scenic trail offers amazing views of the chiseled, terra-cotta-colored Crimson Cliffs (cover photo).

Driving directions: From the Sedona Y (Highways 89A and 179 junction), drive 1.3 miles south on Highway 179 (towards Phoenix) to Morgan Road and turn left. Continue 0.6 miles to the posted trailhead parking lot on the left at the end of the road.

From Bell Rock Boulevard, in the Village of Oak Creek, drive 5.1 miles north to the Morgan Road turnoff on the right.

Hiking directions: Two trails depart from this trailhead. The Broken Arrow Trail leaves from the south side of the parking lot (Hikes 80 and 81). Take the posted Marg's Draw Trail from the north side and cross a wash. Enter the Munds Mountain Wilderness, and wind through a forest of pinyon pines, junipers, and Arizona cypress. Climb a small hill to great red rock vistas of Capitol Butte, Wilson Mountain, and Steamboat Rock. Cross the easy rolling terrain on the west edge of the wilderness, and pass a rock draw on the edge of a 25-foot drop at 0.75 miles. At one mile, as you approach the base of the sculpted Crimson Cliffs, is a posted junction. This is the turn-around spot.

To extend the hike, continue with Hikes 77 or 78. This route can also be hiked as a 2-mile, one-way shuttle with Hike 77.

HIKES 77–79
MARG'S DRAW
NORTH and SOUTH TRAILHEADS
CRIMSON CLIFFS • SNOOPY ROCK

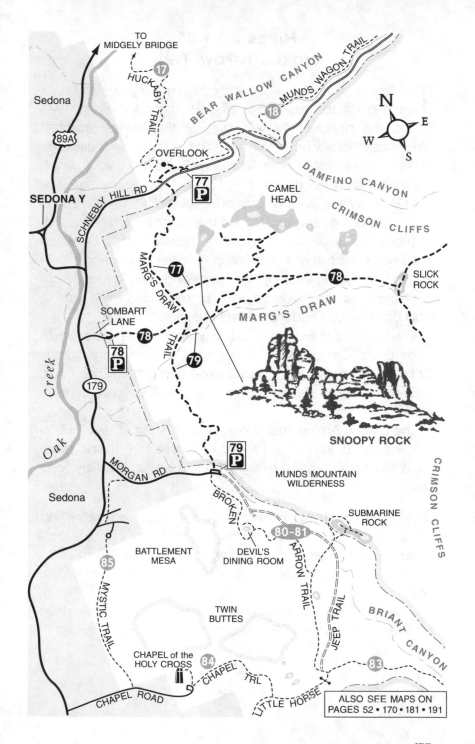

TO
MIDGELY BRIDGE

Sedona

SEDONA Y

89A

HUCKABY TRAIL

17

BEAR WALLOW CANYON

MUNDS WAGON TRAIL

18

N
W E
S

OVERLOOK

SCHNEBLY HILL RD

77
P

CAMEL
HEAD

DAMFINO CANYON

CRIMSON CLIFFS

77

MARG'S DRAW TRAIL

SOMBART
LANE

78

78
P

179

78

79

MARG'S DRAW

78

SLICK
ROCK

SNOOPY ROCK

Creek

Oak

Sedona

MORGAN RD

79
P

MUNDS MOUNTAIN
WILDERNESS

BROKEN

SUBMARINE
ROCK

CRIMSON CLIFFS

85

MYSTIC TRAIL

BATTLEMENT
MESA

DEVIL'S
DINING ROOM

ARROW TRAIL

80-81

JEEP TRAIL

BRIANT CANYON

TWIN
BUTTES

83

CHAPEL of the
HOLY CROSS

84

CHAPEL TRL

CHAPEL ROAD

LITTLE HORSE

ALSO SEE MAPS ON
PAGES 52 • 170 • 181 • 191

Hikes 80 • 81
Broken Arrow Trail

The Broken Arrow Trail leads through a gorgeous red rock basin along the east edge of Battlement Mesa and Twin Buttes. This popular trail, just outside the Munds Mountain Wilderness boundary, leads to three distinct Sedona landmarks—Devil's Dining Room, Submarine Rock, and Chicken Point.

Devil's Dining Room is a 60- to 90-foot deep, cave-like sinkhole with a 30-foot diameter. The sinkhole was created when the roof of an underground limestone cavern collapsed.

Submarine Rock sits in the long, narrow valley between Munds Mountain and Twin Buttes. The bald formation is partially submerged in a sea of Arizona cypress and junipers. From atop the mounded rock are 360-degree views. Walt Disney, who often visited Sedona, named the rock.

Chicken Point is a stunning red rock overlook near the mouth of Briant Canyon, with views of the Twin Butte Spires, Cathedral Rock, Bell Rock, Courthouse Butte, Submarine Rock, Lee Mountain, Munds Mountain, and the multicolored Crimson Cliffs.

The Broken Arrow Trail connects with Marg's Draw Trail to the north (Hike 79) and the Little Horse Trail to the south (Hike 82) for extended hiking. The area is also used by jeep tours.

Driving directions: From the Sedona Y (Highways 89A and 179 junction), drive 1.3 miles south on Highway 179 (towards Phoenix) to Morgan Road and turn left. Continue 0.6 miles to the posted trailhead parking lot at the end of the road on the left.

From Bell Rock Boulevard in the Village of Oak Creek, drive 5.1 miles north to the Morgan Road turnoff on the right.

Hike 80
Broken Arrow Trail to
Devil's Dining Room and Submarine Rock

Hiking distance: 2 miles round trip
Hiking time: 1 hour
Elevation gain: 240 feet
Maps: U.S.G.S. Sedona and Munds Mountain
Beartooth Publishing—Sedona, AZ

map
next page

Driving directions: See page 178.

Hiking directions: Walk south past the trailhead map, and cross the jeep road on the signed footpath. Cairns mark the hiking trail along the north face of Battlement Mesa. Cross the sandstone ledge and wind along the base of the towering red rock formation. The top of Submarine Rock appears to be floating just above the treeline to the southwest. Leave Battlement Mesa behind, and follow the contours of the red rock hills. Drop down to the fenced Devil's Dining Room on the left.

After viewing the sinkhole, continue to the right to a posted junction on a minor ridge. The right fork heads to Chicken Point (Hike 81). Take the left fork towards Submarine Rock and descend, with sweeping views of the Crimson Cliffs, Snoopy Rock, Munds Mountain, Lee Mountain, and Battlement Mesa. At the bottom of the hill, cross a flat rock slab, following cairns to the lower north end. Pick up the red dirt path, and curve clockwise to the east side of the hill to the first close-up view of Submarine Rock and a view into Briant Canyon. Cross the jeep access road, and continue on the footpath to the north end of Submarine Rock. Walk around to the east side of the formation, and traverse the base. Climb the mounded rock, choosing your own route. From atop the rock are sweeping 360-degree vistas.

Hike 81
Broken Arrow Trail to
Devil's Dining Room and Chicken Point

Hiking distance: 3 miles round trip
Hiking time: 1.5 hours
Elevation gain: 300 feet
Maps: U.S.G.S. Sedona and Munds Mountain
      Beartooth Publishing—Sedona, AZ

Driving directions: See page 178.

Hiking directions: Follow the hiking directions for Hike 80 to the Submarine Rock junction. The left fork heads to Submarine Rock (Hike 80). Take the right fork towards Chicken Point and head south. The serpentine path climbs to a ridge, where layers of ridges and draws can be viewed in the surrounding landscape. The forested drainage to the southeast is Briant Canyon. Climb to a smooth rock dome near a circular outcropping called Mushroom Rock. This is a popular spot for touring jeeps and enjoying the panoramic vistas. Continue on the footpath, leaving the knoll, and traverse the hillside beneath the sculpted formations to the rounded red rock knobs of Chicken Point (back cover photo). This is our turn-around spot.

    To hike farther, the trail continues on the Little Horse Trail into Briant Canyon (Hike 84) or can be combined with Hike 82 for a 3-mile, one-way shuttle to the Little Horse Trailhead.

HIKE 80
DEVIL'S DINING ROOM • SUBMARINE ROCK
HIKE 81
DEVIL'S DINING ROOM • CHICKEN POINT
BROKEN ARROW TRAIL

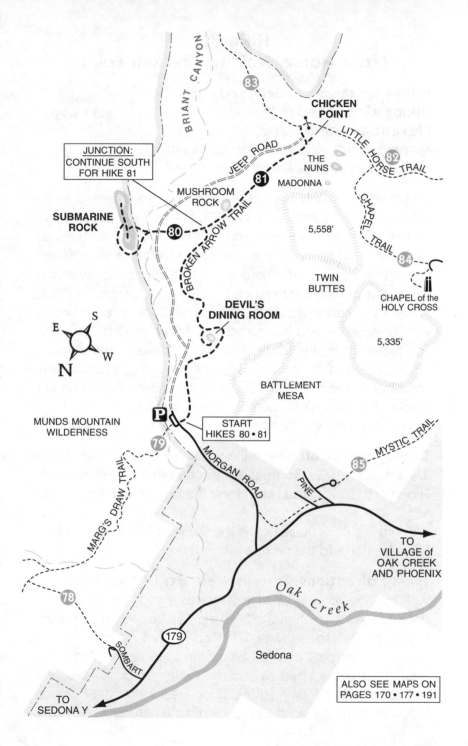

BRIANT CANYON

83

CHICKEN
POINT

LITTLE HORSE TRAIL

82

JUNCTION:
CONTINUE SOUTH
FOR HIKE 81

JEEP ROAD

THE
NUNS

81

MADONNA

MUSHROOM
ROCK

CHAPEL TRAIL

SUBMARINE
ROCK

80

BROKEN ARROW TRAIL

5,558'

84

CHAPEL of the
HOLY CROSS

TWIN
BUTTES

DEVIL'S
DINING ROOM

5,335'

E   S

N   W

BATTLEMENT
MESA

MUNDS MOUNTAIN
WILDERNESS

P

79

START
HIKES 80 • 81

MYSTIC TRAIL

85

MORGAN ROAD

PINE

MARG'S DRAW TRAIL

TO
VILLAGE of
OAK CREEK
AND PHOENIX

78

Oak Creek

179

Sedona

SOMBART

ALSO SEE MAPS ON
PAGES 170 • 177 • 191

TO
SEDONA Y

Hike 82
Little Horse Trail to Chicken Point

Hiking distance: 3 miles round trip

Hiking time: 1.5 hours

Elevation gain: 300 feet

Maps: U.S.G.S. Sedona and Munds Mountain
Beartooth Publishing—Sedona, AZ

map
next page

Summary of hike: The Little Horse Trail meanders through a beautiful draw between Twin Buttes and the West Ridge of Lee Mountain. The trail leads to Chicken Point, a series of large, rounded flat rocks and spectacular red rock vistas (back cover photo). From the bare knob formations are awesome views of the Twin Butte spires, Cathedral Rock, Gibraltar Rock, Bell Rock, Courthouse Butte, Submarine Rock, Lee Mountain, Munds Mountain, and the multicolored Crimson Cliffs. En route to Chicken Point, the scenic trail passes beneath the eroded, sandstone pinnacles of Chapel Spires, Madonna, and The Nuns. The Little Horse Trail connects with the Broken Arrow Trail at Chicken Point (Hike 81). These two trails can be combined for a 3-mile, one-way shuttle hike.

Driving directions: From the Sedona Y (Highways 89A and 179 junction), drive 3.5 miles south on Highway 179 (towards Phoenix) to the posted Little Horse Trailhead parking lot on the left.

From Bell Rock Boulevard in the Village of Oak Creek, drive 2.9 miles north to the parking lot on the right.

Hiking directions: From the east end of the parking lot, walk to a posted trail junction 20 yards ahead. The Mystic Trail (Hike 85) goes to the left. Take the Bell Rock Pathway south (right), parallel to Highway 179. Top a small rise to a signed junction at 0.2 miles. Bear left on the Little Horse Trail, and curve around a small hill. Head east up the wide canyon towards the red rock cliffs of Twin Buttes. Drop into a forest of pinyon pines, Arizona cypress, and junipers to an eroding rock wall.

Bear left, climbing out of the draw to a minor ridge and overlook of the area. Steadily gain elevation, with numerous dips and rises. Cross a slickrock drainage to the base of the vertical red rock wall of Twin Buttes and a junction with the Chapel Trail on the left (Hike 84). Stay right along the base of the towering wall, and pass through a trail gate by red rock mounds. Weave through a maze of awesome formations (back cover photo) to the smooth ledges on Chicken Point, marveling at the sweeping 360-degree vistas. This is the turn-around spot.

To hike farther, the trail continues north as the Broken Arrow Trail and leads to Submarine Rock, the Devil's Dining Room, and the trailhead on Morgan Road (Hikes 80 and 81). A side path, just before reaching Chicken Point, heads into Briant Canyon (Hike 83).

Hike 83
Little Horse Trail to Briant Canyon

Hiking distance: 5 miles round trip
Hiking time: 2.5 hours
Elevation gain: 400 feet
Maps: U.S.G.S. Sedona and Munds Mountain
       Beartooth Publishing—Sedona, AZ

*map
next page*

Summary of hike: Briant Canyon is an isolated draw in an undeveloped, native setting. The forested canyon, within the Munds Mountain Wilderness, is tucked between Lee Mountain and the West Ridge of Lee Mountain. Access to the canyon is from the Little Horse Trail (Hike 82). A side path near Chicken Point enters the mouth of the red-walled canyon to an overlook at trail's end.

Driving directions: Same as Hike 82.

Hiking directions: From the east end of the parking lot, walk to a posted trail junction 20 yards ahead. The Mystic Trail (Hike 85) goes to the left. Take the Bell Rock Pathway south (right), parallel to Highway 179. Top a small rise to a signed junction at 0.2 miles. Bear left on the Little Horse Trail, and curve around a small hill. Head east up the wide canyon towards the red rock cliffs of Twin Buttes. Drop into an evergreen forest, and continue to an eroding rock wall. Bear left, climbing out of the draw to a minor ridge and overlook of the area. Steadily gain elevation while hiking over numerous dips and rises. Cross a slickrock drainage to the base of the vertical red rock wall of Twin Buttes and a junction with the Chapel Trail on the left (Hike 84). Stay to the right along the base of the towering wall. Pass through a trail gate by red rock mounds, and weave through a maze of awesome formations. Just before reaching the summit at Chicken Point, take the distinct side path to the right and curve into Briant Canyon. Walk through the forest on the narrow footpath, and enter the Munds Mountain Wilderness. Wind through the quiet side canyon on the roller-coaster path, heading away from the main hiking route. Follow the west wall of the canyon between Lee Mountain and the West Ridge of Lee Mountain. Cross a few small drainages as you descend to the canyon bottom. Re-climb the west canyon wall, and drop again to the sandy canyon floor. Follow the streambed to a canyon split, where Lee Canyon curves east. Cross the drainage and stay in Briant Canyon to the right in the south canyon fork. Walk across the sloping slick rock mound marked with cairns. Surrounding the trail are red rock walls, spires, and vistas north to Wilson Mountain. The view from this spot is pristine, untouched by development.

HIKE 82
CHICKEN POINT
HIKE 83
BRIANT CANYON
LITTLE HORSE TRAIL

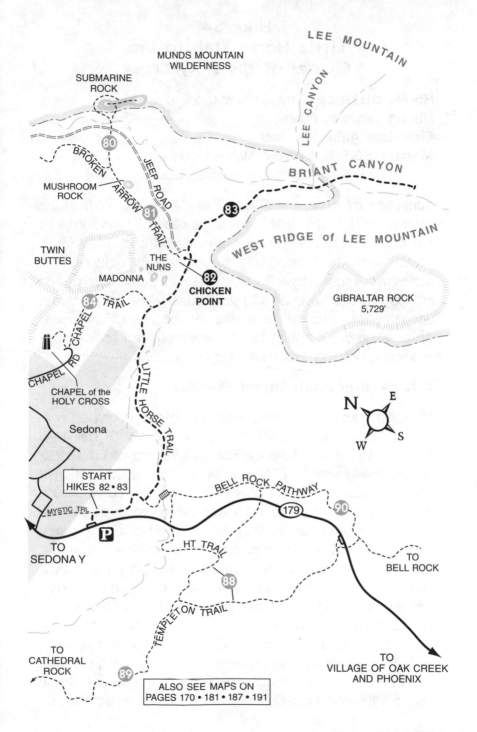

LEE MOUNTAIN

MUNDS MOUNTAIN
WILDERNESS

SUBMARINE
ROCK

LEE CANYON

(80)

BROKEN ARROW TRAIL

JEEP ROAD

MUSHROOM
ROCK

BRIANT CANYON

(81)

(83)

WEST RIDGE of LEE MOUNTAIN

TWIN
BUTTES

THE
NUNS

MADONNA

(84) TRAIL

(82)
CHICKEN
POINT

GIBRALTAR ROCK
5,729'

CHAPEL RD

CHAPEL of the
HOLY CROSS

LITTLE HORSE TRAIL

Sedona

N
E
W
S

START
HIKES 82 • 83

BELL ROCK PATHWAY

MYSTIC TRL

(179)

(90)

P

TO
SEDONA Y

HT TRAIL

TO
BELL ROCK

(88)

TEMPLETON TRAIL

TO
CATHEDRAL
ROCK

(89)

ALSO SEE MAPS ON
PAGES 170 • 181 • 187 • 191

TO
VILLAGE OF OAK CREEK
AND PHOENIX

Hike 84
Little Horse Trail to the
Chapel of the Holy Cross

Hiking distance: 3 miles round trip
Hiking time: 1.5 hours
Elevation gain: 200 feet
Maps: U.S.G.S. Sedona and Munds Mountain
Beartooth Publishing—Sedona, AZ

Summary of hike: The Chapel Trail is a side path off of the Little Horse Trail. The trail follows the base of Twin Buttes to the Chapel of the Holy Cross, considered one of Sedona's power sites. The Chapel, built amidst the red rocks of Twin Buttes, was inspired by a Frank Lloyd Wright design. Completed in 1956, the Sedona landmark rises dramatically from the butte, yet integrates into the landscape. At the chapel is a public observation deck, highlighting the gorgeous red rock buttes, eroded spires, and surrounding terrain.

Driving directions: Same as Hike 82.

Hiking directions: From the east end of the parking lot, walk to a posted trail junction 20 yards ahead. The Mystic Trail (Hike 85) goes to the left. Take the Bell Rock Pathway south (right), parallel to Highway 179. Top a small rise to a signed junction at 0.2 miles. Bear left on the Little Horse Trail, and curve around a small hill. Head east up the wide canyon towards the red rock cliffs of Twin Buttes. Drop into a forest of pinyon pines, Arizona cypress, and junipers to an eroding rock wall. Bear left, climbing out of the draw to a minor ridge and overlook of the area. Steadily gain elevation while hiking over numerous dips and rises. Cross a slickrock drainage to the base of the vertical red rock wall of Twin Buttes and a junction. Leave the Little Horse Trail, and bear left on the Chapel Trail. Follow the sheer, red rock wall along the south base of Twin Buttes and the spire formations. Cross an elevated slick rock drainage on a ledge above a 10-foot drop. Continue along the hillside, perched on the rock shelf above the valley floor. Wind through an open forest on the rolling terrain parallel to Twin Buttes as the Chapel of the Holy Cross, nestled into the cliffs, comes into view. The trail ends at the lower parking lot of the chapel. Walk uphill to the chapel and the observation deck on the right.

CHAPEL of the HOLY CROSS

TO BRIANT CANYON

81 83

TWIN BUTTES
5,558'

MADONNA

CHICKEN POINT

THE NUNS 82

CHAPEL TRAIL

5,335'

MYSTIC TRAIL

OVERLOOK

CHAPEL

85

CHAPEL ROAD

TO SEDONA Y

ANTELOPE DR

LITTLE HORSE TRAIL

N E W S

Sedona

TO BELL ROCK

179

ROCK TRAIL 90

MYSTIC TRL BELL

P

TO VILLAGE of OAK CREEK AND PHOENIX

HT TRAIL

ALSO SEE MAPS ON PAGES 170 • 185 • 191

BACK O' BEYOND ROAD

CHAPEL of the HOLY CROSS
LITTLE HORSE TRAIL

Hike 85
Mystic Trail from Chapel Road

Hiking distance: 2 miles round trip
Hiking time: 1 hour
Elevation gain: 200 feet
Maps: U.S.G.S. Sedona
Beartooth Publishing—Sedona, AZ

map next page

Summary of hike: The Mystic Trail is a connector trail between the Bell Rock Pathway (Hike 90) and the Broken Arrow Trail (Hike 81). The trail travels across a gently rolling terrain beneath the towering west wall of Twin Buttes, offering great views of Wilson Mountain to the north and Cathedral Rock to the west. It is a short easy trail with quick access and magnificent vistas. The trail can also be hiked as part of a loop around Twin Buttes (Hike 86).

Driving directions: From the Sedona Y (Highways 89A and 179 junction), drive 2.8 miles south on Highway 179 (towards Phoenix) to Chapel Road and turn left. Continue 0.35 miles to the posted trailhead on the left, across from Antelope Drive. Park along the shoulder of the road in the narrow pullout on the left by the trailhead. There are additional spaces a short distance ahead on the left.

From Bell Rock Boulevard in the Village of Oak Creek, drive 3.6 miles north to the Chapel Road turnoff on the right.

A second trailhead is located at the north end of the hike. It is accessed from Pine Drive, 1.6 miles south of the Sedona Y and 4.8 miles north of Bell Rock Boulevard. From Pine Drive, head 100 yards to Pine Knolls. Turn right and park in the cul-de-sac at the end of the road.

Hiking directions: The Mystic Trail's southernmost trailhead begins at the Little Horse Trailhead (Hikes 82–84). However, this hike eliminates walking through the residential area and begins on Chapel Road instead. From Chapel Road, pass the trailhead map and head north through a forest of pinyon pines, Arizona cypress, and junipers. Follow the rolling terrain along the west base of Twin Buttes, with views of Cathedral Rock to the west and Table Top Mountain to the northwest. As you near the northwest corner of Twin Buttes, cross over a rise to vistas from West Sedona to Wilson Mountain. Descend past Twin Buttes to a view of Snoopy Rock, Crimson Ridge, Battlement Mesa, and Munds Mountain. Continue losing elevation to the end of the trail at a cul-de-sac on Pine Knolls Drive. Return along the same route, or continue with Hike 86.

Hike 86
Twin Buttes—Battlement Mesa Loop
BROKEN ARROW—LITTLE HORSE—CHAPEL—MYSTIC TRAILS

Hiking distance: 5 mile loop
Hiking time: 2.5 hours
Elevation gain: 300 feet
Maps: U.S.G.S. Sedona and Munds Mountain
       Beartooth Publishing—Sedona, AZ

map next page

Summary of hike: This hike makes a loop around Twin Buttes and Battlement Mesa, combining four trails and a variety of scenery. The hike begins on the Broken Arrow Trail and leads through a gorgeous red rock basin to an overlook at Chicken Point. En route, the trail passes Devil's Dining Room, a 60- to 90-foot deep sinkhole, and detours to Submarine Rock, a bald rock formation partially submerged in a sea of trees. The Little Horse Trail descends along the red rock wall of Twin Buttes, with vistas of Cathedral Rock, Gibraltar Rock, Bell Rock, and Courthouse Butte. The Chapel Trail follows the base of Twin Buttes to the Chapel of the Holy Cross and an overlook, considered one of Sedona's power sites. The Mystic Trail returns beneath the towering west wall of Twin Buttes.

Driving directions: Same as Hike 80, page 178.

Hiking directions: Take the signed Broken Arrow Trail and cross the jeep road. Cairns mark the hiking trail along the north face of Battlement Mesa. Cross the ledge along the base of the towering red rock formation. Leave Battlement Mesa behind, and follow the contours of the red rock hills. Drop down to Devil's Dining Room on the left. After viewing the sinkhole, continue to the right to a posted junction on a minor ridge. The left fork detours to Submarine Rock (Hike 80). Take the right fork towards Chicken Point and head south. The serpentine path climbs to a ridge with views of the surrounding landscape. The smooth, circular rock dome to the left is Mushroom Rock. Leave the knoll and traverse the hillside beneath the sculpted formations to the rounded rock knobs of Chicken Point. Descend from the overlook through the draw, and pass through a trail gate. Steadily descend along the base of Twin Buttes to a posted junction. Bear right on the Chapel Trail, and follow the sheer, red rock wall of Twin Buttes. Cross an elevated slick rock drainage, perched on the rock shelf above the valley floor. The trail ends at the lower parking lot of the Chapel of the Holy Cross. Detour uphill to the right and visit the chapel and overlook. Return back to Chapel Road, and head downhill 0.4 miles on the road to the posted Mystic Trail on the right. Head north on the rolling terrain along the west base of Twin Buttes. Near the northwest corner of Twin Buttes, cross over a rise and descend to the end of the trail at a cul-de-sac on Pine Knolls Drive. Walk to Pine Drive at the end of the block . Bear left a half block to the posted bike trail, just shy of Highway 179. Head north on the red dirt path, parallel to the highway, and cross Painted Canyon Drive. A short distance ahead, curve right onto Morgan Road. Follow Morgan Road a half mile, completing the loop at the trailhead parking lot.

HIKE 85
MYSTIC TRAIL
HIKE 86
TWIN BUTTES–
BATTLEMENT MESA LOOP

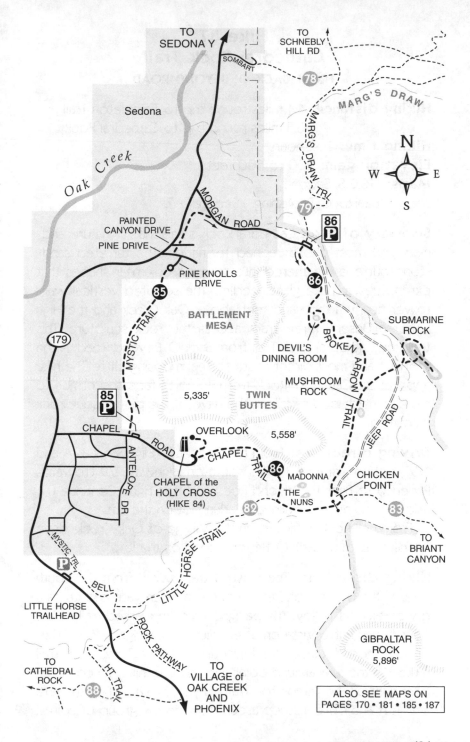

Hike 87
Cathedral Rock Trail
FROM BACK O' BEYOND ROAD

Hiking distance: 1.4 miles round trip to Templeton Trail
3.5 miles round trip to Cathedral Rock
Hiking time: 1—2 hours
Elevation gain: 200 to 600 feet
Maps: U.S.G.S. Sedona
Beartooth Publishing—Sedona, AZ

Summary of hike: Cathedral Rock is Sedona's signature land-mark and most photographed formation. The turreted sand-stone butte is weathered into majestic columnar shapes that extend upward like giant needles. The sculpted vertical walls tower nearly a thousand feet above Oak Creek and the High Sonoran Desert. Three trails access the rock sculpture. This trail, the Cathedral Rock Trail from Back O' Beyond Road, is the shortest and most direct route to the imposing cliffs. The hike approaches Cathedral Rock from its north face and climbs to a crescent-shaped saddle in the nave of the picturesque rock monument.

Driving directions: From the Sedona Y (Highways 89A and 179 junction), drive 3.3 miles south on Highway 179 (towards Phoenix) to Back O' Beyond Road and turn right. Continue 0.6 miles to the posted trailhead parking lot on the left.
From Bell Rock Boulevard in the Village of Oak Creek, drive 3.1 miles north to Back O' Beyond Road on the left.

Hiking directions: The posted trail leaves from the south side of the parking lot. Pass through an open gate and cross a dry creek bed. Follow the designated cairn-marked trail to the Courthouse Butte Vista on a red slick rock ledge at 0.6 miles. Climb a short distance to a T-junction with the Templeton Trail (Hike 89) the turn-around point for a shorter hike. To continue, bear right on the Templeton Trail 40 yards to a trail on the left. Bear left and make a steep ascent toward the group of spires.

This section requires some rock scrambling. Use caution and be mindful of your own hiking capabilities. The trail ends on a saddle between the spires, with panoramic vistas in every direction.

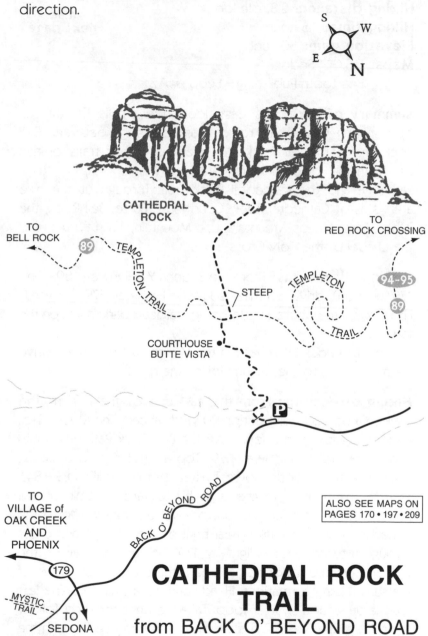

CATHEDRAL ROCK

TO BELL ROCK

89

TEMPLETON TRAIL

TO RED ROCK CROSSING

TEMPLETON TRAIL

94-95

89

STEEP

COURTHOUSE BUTTE VISTA

P

TO VILLAGE of OAK CREEK AND PHOENIX

BACK O' BEYOND ROAD

ALSO SEE MAPS ON PAGES 170 • 197 • 209

179

MYSTIC TRAIL

TO SEDONA

CATHEDRAL ROCK TRAIL
from BACK O' BEYOND ROAD

Hike 88
HT—Templeton—Bell Rock Pathway Loop

Hiking distance: 2.8 mile loop
Hiking time: 1.5 hours
Elevation gain: 50 feet
Maps: U.S.G.S. Sedona
Beartooth Publishing—Sedona, AZ

map
next page

Summary of hike: This easy loop hike strolls through an open rolling basin with rocky wash crossings between Bell Rock and Cathedral Rock. A variety of other trails branch off from the loop, including the Little Horse Trail, Bell Rock Pathway, and the Cathedral Rock Trail. Throughout the hike are vistas of Cathedral Rock, Courthouse Butte, Bell Rock, the Rabbit Ears, Munds Mountain, Lee Mountain, Twin Buttes, and the Chapel of the Holy Cross.

Driving directions: From the Sedona Y (Highways 89A and 179 junction), drive 3.5 miles south on Highway 179 (towards Phoenix) to the posted Little Horse Trailhead parking lot on the left.

From Bell Rock Boulevard in the Village of Oak Creek, drive 2.9 miles north to the parking lot on the right.

Hiking directions: From the east end of the parking lot, walk to a posted trail junction 20 yards ahead. The Mystic Trail (Hike 85) goes to the left. Take the Bell Rock Pathway south (right), parallel to Highway 179. Top a small rise to a signed junction with the Little Horse Trail at 0.2 miles (Hikes 82—84). Stay to the right and wind downhill towards prominent Bell Rock. Cross a wooden footbridge over a rocky gorge to the signed HT Trail at 0.3 miles. Bear right on the HT Trail, and cross through a tunnel under Highway 179. Pick up the trail on the left, and climb a minor ridge, where there are great views of the surrounding formations. Head south to a trail fork. The left fork returns for a shorter loop. Take the right fork and follow the rock cairns west. Cross a drainage and weave through the open forest to a T-junction with the Templeton Trail. The right fork leads to Cathedral Rock (Hike 89). For this hike, take the left fork and weave through pinyon pines and Arizona cypress. Cross a small ridge and head towards prominent Courthouse Butte. Follow the west edge of a draw and cross a drainage. Continue east and descend to Highway 179. Cross through a rock tunnel under the highway, and follow the trail 100 yards to a T-junction with the Bell Rock Pathway. The right fork leads to Bell Rock (Hikes 90—92). Take the left fork and head north on the wide path. The trail parallels the west face of Lee Mountain, with sweeping curves and gentle dips and rises. Complete the loop at the junction with the HT Trail. Cross the footbridge and return to the trailhead.

Hike 89
Templeton Trail to Cathedral Rock

Hiking distance: 7 miles round trip
Hiking time: 3.5 hours
Elevation gain: 250 feet
Maps: U.S.G.S. Sedona
　　　Beartooth Publishing—Sedona, AZ

map
next page

Summary of hike: Cathedral Rock, long considered a magnetic energy vortex and healing site, has three access trails. The Templeton Trail begins from the Bell Rock Pathway (north of Bell Rock) and approaches the east face of the Cathedral Rock, connecting the two popular formations. The hike traverses a redrock shelf on the shoulder of the weathered sandstone monument. The wide path curves around the north and west faces of Cathedral Rock, descending to Oak Creek and the Baldwin Trail near Red Rock Crossing (Hikes 94 and 95).

Driving directions: From the Sedona Y (Highways 89A and 179 junction), drive 4.8 miles south on Highway 179 (towards Phoenix) to a large pullout on the right side of the road.
　　　From Bell Rock Boulevard in the Village of Oak Creek, drive 1.6 miles north to the large pullout on the left.

Hiking directions: Take the walking path into the forest, and curve left (south) 30 yards to a trail sign by a rock tunnel leading under Highway 179. Take the Templeton Trail to the right, away from the highway. Stroll through an open pine and cypress forest, dropping into and crossing a rocky drainage. Ascend a hillside, cross a small ridge, and again descend into the valley. Pass a posted junction with the HT Trail on the right, leading to the Little Horse Trailhead (Hike 88). The trail drops into the lush valley to the base of Cathedral Rock and curves north along the edge of the red rock cliffs. Traverse the rock shelf, perched above the valley but beneath the weathered columnar spires. Curve around to the north face of Cathedral Rock to a posted junction at 2.4 miles. The Cathedral Rock Trail bears right to the trailhead at Back O' Beyond Road (Hike 87). Continue 40 yards to the left fork of the Cathedral Rock Trail, which climbs to a saddle between the spires. Stay on the rock ledge to the northernmost point of Cathedral Rock. Make a horseshoe left bend, cross a ravine, and wind sharply downhill to the forested valley floor at Oak Creek. Wind through the valley bottom between the red rock cliffs and the south banks of Oak Creek to a posted junction at the end of the Templeton Trail. The Baldwin Trail (Hike 95) goes left (south). Continue straight, parallel to Oak Creek, to Red Rock Crossing at the end of Verde Valley School Road.

HIKE 88
HT–TEMPLETON–
BELL ROCK PATHWAY
LOOP
HIKE 89
TEMPLETON TRAIL
to CATHEDRAL ROCK

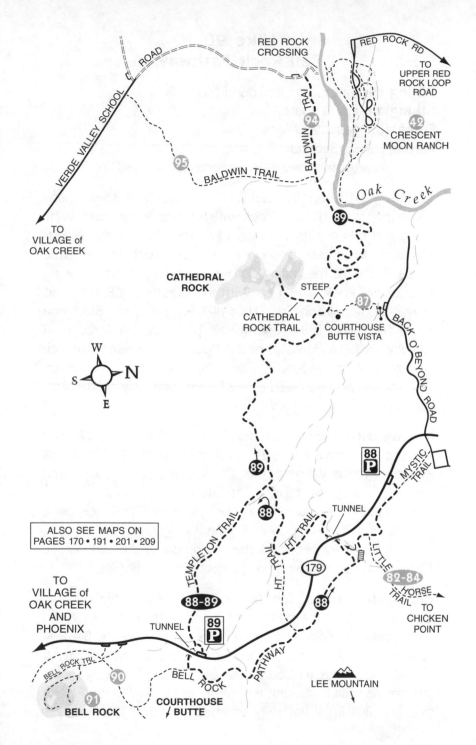

RED ROCK CROSSING

RED ROCK RD

TO UPPER RED ROCK LOOP ROAD

94 BALDWIN TRAIL

42 CRESCENT MOON RANCH

Oak Creek

VERDE VALLEY SCHOOL ROAD

95 BALDWIN TRAIL

TO VILLAGE of OAK CREEK

89

CATHEDRAL ROCK

STEEP

87

CATHEDRAL ROCK TRAIL

COURTHOUSE BUTTE VISTA

BACK O' BEYOND ROAD

W
S — N
E

89

88 P

MYSTIC TRAIL

ALSO SEE MAPS ON PAGES 170 • 191 • 201 • 209

TEMPLETON TRAIL

88

HT TRAIL

HT TRAIL

TUNNEL

179

TO VILLAGE of OAK CREEK AND PHOENIX

88-89

89 P

TUNNEL

88

82-84

LITTLE HORSE TRAIL

TO CHICKEN POINT

BELL ROCK TRL

90

BELL ROCK

PATHWAY

LEE MOUNTAIN

91 BELL ROCK

COURTHOUSE BUTTE

Hike 90
Bell Rock Pathway

Hiking distance: 7 miles round trip
Hiking time: 3.5 hours
Elevation gain: 200 feet
Maps: U.S.G.S. Sedona
Beartooth Publishing — Sedona, AZ

Summary of hike: The Bell Rock Pathway is a 3.5-mile trail linking the Village of Oak Creek with Sedona. The smooth, wide hiking and biking path parallels Highway 179 and the Munds Mountain Wilderness boundary from Bell Rock to the Little Horse Trailhead. The rolling pathway curves around the west base of Bell Rock, linking up with the Courthouse Butte Loop (Hike 92), Templeton Trail (Hike 89), HT Trail (Hike 88), Little Horse Trail (Hike 82-84), and Mystic Trail (Hike 85). Throughout the hike are fantastic vistas of Bell Rock, Courthouse Butte, Lee Mountain, Munds Mountain, Cathedral Rock, and Twin Buttes. This trail can also be hiked as a 3.5-mile, one-way shuttle with Hike 82.

Driving directions: From the Sedona Y (Highways 89A and 179 junction), drive 6.2 miles south on Highway 179 (towards Phoenix) into the Village of Oak Creek. Turn left into the posted Bell Rock Vista parking lot on the left.
From Bell Rock Boulevard in the Village of Oak Creek, drive 0.2 miles north to the parking lot on the right.
For a one-way hike, park the shuttle car at the Little Horse Trailhead, following the driving directions for Hike 88.

Hiking directions: Take the posted Bell Rock Pathway from the south end of the parking lot. Curve left on the wide dirt path, and pass two junctions on the right with the Big Park Loop (Hike 93). The second junction, at the southwest corner of Bell Rock, leads to Courthouse Butte (Hike 92). Stay to the left on the main trail along the west side of Bell Rock. At one mile, the Bell Rock Pathway reaches a posted junction with the Bell Rock Trail at the northwest corner of Bell Rock. Stay on the main trail and curve north. Pass the Courthouse Butte Trail on the right (Hike 92) and the Templeton Trail on the left (Hike 89). The path steadily dips and rises with wide, sweeping curves and great views of Cathedral Rock and Twin Buttes. Pass a junction with the HT Trail (Hike 88) on the left, and cross a wooden footbridge over a rocky gorge. Head uphill, passing the Little Horse Trail on the right to a junction with the Mystic Trail at the Little Horse Trailhead parking lot (Hike 82), where the Bell Rock Pathway ends.

TO SEDONA

BACK O' BEYOND ROAD

85 MYSTIC

P

82-84

LITTLE HORSE

LITTLE TRAIL

TUNNEL

TO CATHEDRAL ROCK

89

HT TRL

HT TRL

BELL ROCK PATHWAY

GIBRALTAR ROCK 5,896'

TEMPLETON

88

TRAIL

CATHEDRAL ROCK

TUNNEL

MUNDS MOUNTAIN WILDERNESS

COURTHOUSE BUTTE

DOME

92

N

W ⊕ E

S

91

BELL ROCK

COURTHOUSE BUTTE

TRAIL

BELL ROCK TRAIL

92

BELL ROCK PATHWAY

BIG PARK LOOP

179

BIG PARK

LOOP

BELL ROCK VISTA

P

93

BIG PARK LOOP

BELL ROCK BOULEVARD

Village of Oak Creek

ARROWHEAD CYN DIABLO

PINON WOODS DR

ALSO SEE MAPS ON PAGES 170 • 185 • 197 • 201

BELL ROCK PATHWAY

Hike 91
Bell Rock Trail

Hiking distance: 1—3 miles round trip
Hiking time: 30 minutes to 1.5 hours
Elevation gain: 100 to 400 feet
Maps: U.S.G.S. Sedona
      Beartooth Publishing—Sedona, AZ

Summary of hike: Bell Rock is the prominent bell-shaped landmark on the north end of the Village of Oak Creek. Geologists classify the beautiful red rock sculpture as a butte. The formation is one of Sedona's spiritual vortex centers. Many believe the 550-foot formation energizes and calms those upon its slopes. Due to its close proximity to Highway 179, the popular Bell Rock hike is not a backcountry experience. It is a leisurely, stairstep climb up and around the dynamic slick rock slopes.

Driving directions: Same as Hike 90—park in the Bell Rock Vista parking lot.

At the northwest corner of Bell Rock are two additional (and shorter) access routes. There are two pullouts on each side of Highway 179 located 5.1—5.3 miles south from the Sedona Y and 1.3—1.5 miles north of Bell Rock Boulevard.

Hiking directions: Take the posted Bell Rock Pathway from the south end of the parking lot. Curve left on the wide dirt path bordered by spindly pines, brushy juniper trees, and prickly pear cactus. Pass two junctions on the right with the Big Park Loop (Hike 93). The second junction, at the southwest corner of Bell Rock, leads to Courthouse Butte (Hike 92). Stay to the left on the main trail along the west side of Bell Rock. At one mile, the Bell Rock Pathway reaches the northwest corner of Bell Rock by two connecting trails off of Highway 179. The posted Bell Rock Trail leaves the Bell Rock Pathway and heads up to a rock ledge on the northwest corner of the formation. From the ledge are endless hiking choices. You may climb the conical formation to a sloping shelf or encircle the weathered formation on one of its shelf-like rings. The footing can be challenging along the upper layers, so use caution and common sense.

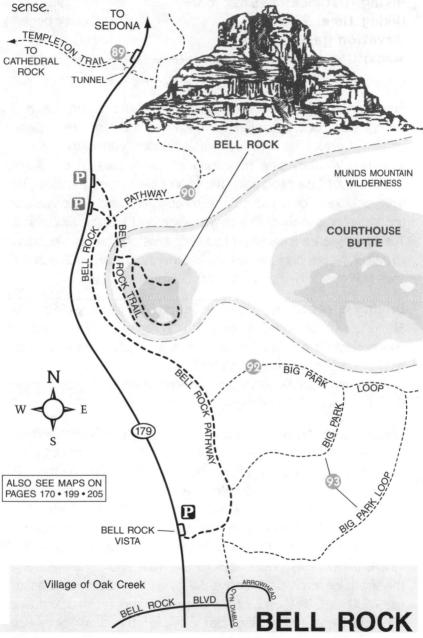

TO SEDONA

TO CATHEDRAL ROCK

TEMPLETON TRAIL

89

TUNNEL

BELL ROCK

MUNDS MOUNTAIN WILDERNESS

P

P

PATHWAY 90

BELL ROCK

BELL ROCK TRAIL

COURTHOUSE BUTTE

N
W E
S

BELL ROCK PATHWAY

92 BIG PARK LOOP

BIG PARK

93

BIG PARK LOOP

179

ALSO SEE MAPS ON PAGES 170 • 199 • 205

P

BELL ROCK VISTA

Village of Oak Creek

ARROWHEAD

Cyn DIABLO

BELL ROCK BLVD

BELL ROCK

Hike 92
Courthouse Butte Loop

Hiking distance: 4.25 mile loop
Hiking time: 2 hours
Elevation gain: 250 feet
Maps: U.S.G.S. Sedona and Munds Mountain
　　　Beartooth Publishing—Sedona, AZ

map
next page

Summary of hike: Courthouse Butte is the enormous and stately red rock monolith on the north end of the Village of Oak Creek. The massive butte resides within the Munds Mountain Wilderness a few hundred yards east of Bell Rock and west of Lee Mountain. The loop hike circles the base of Bell Rock and Courthouse Butte through dry red rock washes and slick rock shelves in a pinyon pine and juniper woodland. The parking area is usually filled with cars and people headed to Bell Rock. Beyond the Bell Rock Pathway, the crowds and the sound of the highway will be left behind.

Driving directions: From the Sedona Y (Highways 89A and 179 junction), drive 6.2 miles south on Highway 179 (towards Phoenix) into the Village of Oak Creek. Turn left into the posted Bell Rock Vista parking lot on the left.

From Bell Rock Boulevard in the Village of Oak Creek, drive 0.2 miles north to the parking lot on the right.

Hiking directions: Take the posted Bell Rock Pathway from the south end of the parking lot. Curve left on the red dirt path to a junction with the Big Park Loop (Hike 93). Stay to the left on the main trail toward Bell Rock. At a half mile, the trail reaches a junction at the southwest corner of Bell Rock. Leave the wide Bell Rock Pathway, and bear right on the footpath. Follow the cairn-marked path toward Courthouse Butte. Pass a junction where the Big Park Loop goes to the right, and continue along the south base of Courthouse Butte, with sweeping vistas of Lee Mountain. Descend into and cross a red slick rock draw. Curve left and follow the east edge of the draw between

Courthouse Butte and Lee Mountain. Leave the narrow canyon bottom and head uphill, surrounded by magnificent formations. Enter the Munds Mountain Wilderness, and cross a wide slab of rock, marked with cairns. Pass a circular red rock knob, and skirt the base of the dome-shaped outcrop. (A side path on the right makes an easy ascent to the outcrop's summit.) The undulating main trail winds through an open forest along the north base of Courthouse Butte to a T-junction with the Bell Rock Pathway. The right fork heads north toward the Little Horse Trail (Hikes 82—84). Bear left along the base of Bell Rock, passing trails leading up Bell Rock (Hike 91) and access paths from Highway 179. Continue on the signed Bell Rock Pathway on the west edge of Bell Rock, parallel to the highway. Complete the loop and return a half mile to the trailhead.

Hike 93
Big Park Loop

Hiking distance: 2 mile loop
Hiking time: 1 hour
Elevation gain: 100 feet
Maps: U.S.G.S. Sedona and Munds Mountain
       Beartooth Publishing—Sedona, AZ

map
next page

Summary of hike: The Big Park Loop is an easy 2.5-mile, double-loop trail in the Village of Oak Creek. The arid terrain on the south side of easily recognized Bell Rock and Courthouse Butte is filled with prickly pear, yucca cacti, pinyon pines, and junipers. The hike begins on the Bell Rock Pathway and loops through the open grasslands under the shadow of Bell Rock, Courthouse Butte, and Lee Mountain.

Driving directions: From the Sedona Y (Highways 89A and 179 junction), drive 6.2 miles south on Highway 179 (towards Phoenix) into the Village of Oak Creek. Turn left into the posted Bell Rock Vista parking lot on the left.
    From Bell Rock Boulevard in the Village of Oak Creek, drive 0.2 miles north to the parking lot on the right.

Hiking directions: Take the posted Bell Rock Pathway from the south end of the parking lot. Curve left, directly toward Courthouse Butte. At 150 yards is a posted junction. Leave the Bell Rock Pathway, and bear right on the Big Park Loop. Wind down to a slickrock slab. Cross the slab and head north toward prominent Bell Rock. Curve right and climb out of the juniper and pine grove to an open grassland with great views of Courthouse Butte and Lee Mountain. Continue to a T-junction at the south base of the vertical-walled butte. The left fork leads to Bell Rock. Go to the right, staying on the Big Park Loop and skirting the base of Courthouse Butte. Cross a small gully and climb again to the open meadows and a junction with a narrow footpath on the right. Bear right and head south on a slightly downhill grade. (If this junction is missed, the trail begins to descend into a forested draw between Courthouse Butte and Lee Mountain on the Courthouse Butte Loop—Hike 93.) Continue south toward the homes. As you near the homes, curve right and drop into, and climb back out of, a forested drainage. At the next junction, bear right and walk 100 yards, completing the loop. Return to the left.

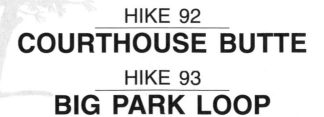

HIKE 92
COURTHOUSE BUTTE
HIKE 93
BIG PARK LOOP

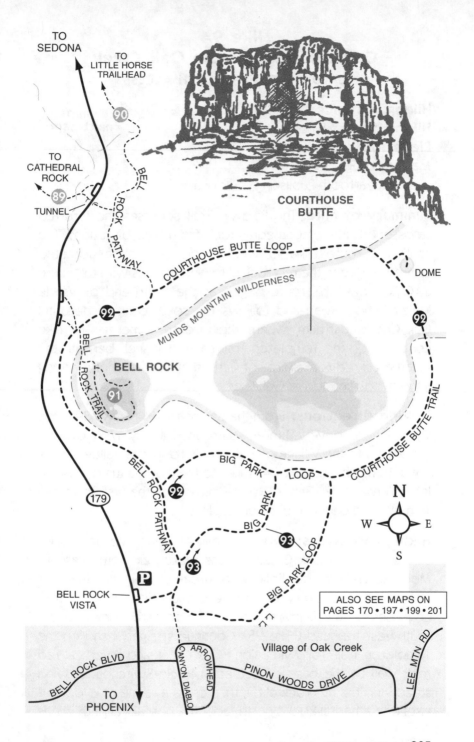

TO
SEDONA

TO
LITTLE HORSE
TRAILHEAD

90

TO
CATHEDRAL
ROCK

89

TUNNEL

BELL ROCK PATHWAY

COURTHOUSE BUTTE LOOP

MUNDS MOUNTAIN WILDERNESS

COURTHOUSE BUTTE

DOME

92

92

BELL ROCK

BELL ROCK TRAIL

91

COURTHOUSE BUTTE TRAIL

BIG PARK LOOP

BELL ROCK PATHWAY

92

BIG PARK LOOP

93

BIG PARK LOOP

93

N
W E
S

(179)

P

BELL ROCK VISTA

ALSO SEE MAPS ON
PAGES 170 • 197 • 199 • 201

Village of Oak Creek

ARROWHEAD

CANYON DIABLO

BELL ROCK BLVD

PINON WOODS DRIVE

LEE MTN RD

TO
PHOENIX

Hike 94
Cathedral Rock from Oak Creek
BALDWIN TRAIL—NORTH ACCESS

Hiking distance: 3 miles round trip

Hiking time: 1.5 hours

map
next page

Elevation gain: 200 feet

Maps: U.S.G.S. Sedona
Beartooth Publishing—Sedona, AZ

Summary of hike: The Baldwin Trail accesses the turreted sandstone butte of Cathedral Rock from two directions. The southwest route (Hike 95) winds through a beautiful forested canyon between the red rock cliffs and merges with this route at Oak Creek. This route begins at the north end of Verde Valley School Road and follows the south bank of beautiful Oak Creek upstream, where the two trails merge. The hike continues on the Templeton Trail to a rock shelf beneath the weathered red rock spires of Cathedral Rock, gracefully rising a thousand feet above Oak Creek.

Driving directions: From the Sedona Y (Highways 89A and 179 junction), drive 7.2 miles south on Highway 179 (towards Phoenix), into the Village of Oak Creek, to Verde Valley School Road. Turn right and drive 4.1 miles to the posted turnoff on the left. (Verde Valley School Road is paved for the first 3.6 miles.) Turn left and park in the lot on the left.

Hiking directions: Walk 0.2 miles down Verde Valley School Road to Oak Creek, across the creek from Crescent Moon Ranch (Hike 42). Follow the creek upstream to the right on a red rock shelf. At a half mile is a junction. The right fork continues on the Baldwin Trail up the forested draw to the southwest trailhead (Hike 95). Continue straight ahead on the Templeton Trail, following along Oak Creek and a vertical red rock wall to the base of Cathedral Rock. Switchbacks wind steeply up the red rock cliffs, then cross a ravine to a lookout vista on Cathedral Rock's north face. The near-level path winds along the contours of Cathedral Rock on a red rock shelf. Vistas open up across Highway 179 to Courthouse Butte, Bell Rock, Crimson Ridge, Munds Mountain, and Lee Mountain. At 1.4 miles, the trail reaches two junctions (40 yards apart) with the Cathedral Rock Trail (Hike 87). This is our turn-around spot.

To continue hiking from the junction, the first (southward) path ascends the rock formation to a saddle between the Cathedral Rock spires. The second (northward) path returns to the trailhead at Back O' Beyond Road. The Templeton Trail continues along the east side of Cathedral Rock, crosses the valley to Highway 179, and connects to Bell Rock (Hikes 89 and 91).

Hike 95
Baldwin Trail to Cathedral Rock
SOUTH ACCESS

Hiking distance: 5 miles round trip
Hiking time: 2.5 hours
Elevation gain: 200 feet
Maps: U.S.G.S. Sedona
      Beartooth Publishing—Sedona, AZ

map
next page

Summary of hike: The Baldwin Trail accesses Cathedral Rock from its west face. The trail begins from two separate trailheads off of Verde Valley School Road. This hike follows the south route, winding through a beautiful forested draw between the red rock cliffs of Cathedral Rock and a rounded 4,400-foot red butte. The route merges with the northern Baldwin Trail at Oak Creek (Hike 94). The hike continues on the Templeton Trail to Cathedral Rock, climbing up to the isolated red rock butte to the base of the formation. The majestic rounded towers and pointy spires gracefully ascend upward for a thousand feet above the surrounding desert terrain.

Driving directions: From the Sedona Y (Highways 89A and 179 junction), drive 7.2 miles south on Highway 179 (towards Phoenix), into the Village of Oak Creek, to Verde Valley School Road. Turn right and drive 4.1 miles to the posted Turkey Creek

Trail turnoff on the left. (Verde Valley School Road is paved for the first 3.6 miles.) Turn left and park in the lot on the left.

Hiking directions: Walk 0.15 miles back up Verde Valley School Road to the posted trailhead on the left. Take the old jeep road east towards the southwest corner of Cathedral Rock. Enter a cypress grove and follow the undulating red dirt trail directly towards, and in full view of, the massive red rock formation. As you near Cathedral Rock, curve left and parallel the formation into a beautiful little canyon. Descend to the north, following the cairns through the narrow red rock canyon. At the northwest corner of Cathedral Rock is a T-junction on the banks of Oak Creek. The left fork is the northern Baldwin Trail (Hike 94), which follows Oak Creek back to Verde Valley School Road. Take the right fork on the Templeton Trail. Walk along Oak Creek and a vertical red rock wall to the base of Cathedral Rock. Climb sharply up the north side of Cathedral Rock on a winding footpath to a rock shelf on the shoulder of the monument. At 2.5 miles, the trail reaches two junctions (40 yards apart) with the Cathedral Rock Trail (Hike 87). This is our turn-around spot.

To continue hiking from the junction, the first (southward) path ascends the sculpted rock formation to a saddle between the spires. The second (northward) path returns to the trailhead at Back O' Beyond Road (Hike 87). The Templeton Trail continues along the east side of Cathedral Rock, crosses the valley to Highway 179, and connects to Bell Rock (Hikes 89 and 91).

HIKES 94–95
CATHEDRAL ROCK from OAK CREEK • BALDWIN TRAIL
NORTH ACCESS—SOUTH ACCESS

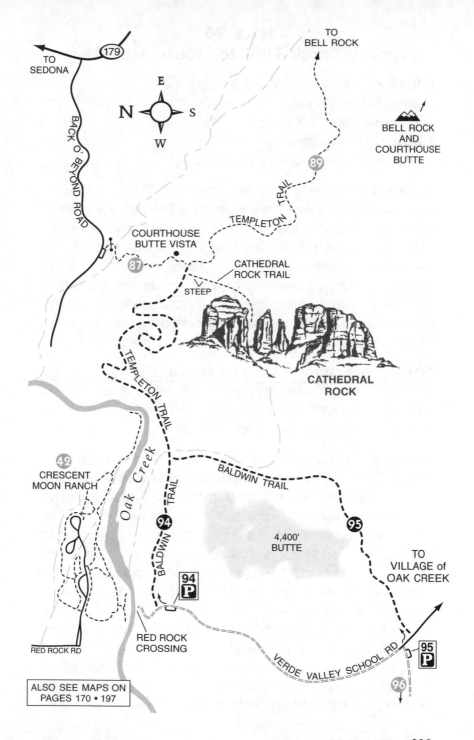

TO
BELL ROCK

TO
SEDONA

179

BELL ROCK
AND
COURTHOUSE
BUTTE

E
N   S
W

BACK O' BEYOND ROAD

89

COURTHOUSE
BUTTE VISTA

TEMPLETON TRAIL

87

CATHEDRAL
ROCK TRAIL

STEEP

TEMPLETON TRAIL

CATHEDRAL
ROCK

Oak Creek

42
CRESCENT
MOON RANCH

BALDWIN TRAIL

BALDWIN TRAIL

4,400'
BUTTE

95

TO
VILLAGE of
OAK CREEK

94

94
P

95
P

RED ROCK RD

RED ROCK
CROSSING

VERDE VALLEY SCHOOL RD

96

ALSO SEE MAPS ON
PAGES 170 • 197

Hike 96
Turkey Creek Trail to House Mountain

Hiking distance: 6 miles round trip
Hiking time: 3 hours
Elevation gain: 1,000 feet
Maps: U.S.G.S. Sedona
  Beartooth Publishing—Sedona, AZ

Summary of hike: House Mountain is a large 5,127-foot mountain south of Red Rock State Park. The mountain, named for its large wall-like lava outcrops, is an extinct volcano with an eroded circular caldera. The Turkey Creek Trail is an old road that winds through a pinyon and juniper forest along a dry creek bed. The trail parallels House Mountain and ascends its north face to a saddle on the rim of the volcanic depression. Side paths lead up to the summit and into the caldera. It is a lightly used trail, offering solitude in a scenic area.

Driving directions: Follow the driving directions for Hike 95 to the Turkey Creek Trail turnoff. Turn left and continue 0.5 miles to a road split. Take the left fork 100 yards to the posted trailhead parking area on the left.

Hiking directions: Pass the rock barrier and take the wide Turkey Creek Trail south towards the mountains. Follow the cairn-marked path over a small rise with sweeping views. Continue to an unsigned trail fork at a quarter mile. Stay on the Turkey Creek Trail to the right, and gradually drop down into the forested valley, surrounded by red rock formations. Meander through the basin, crossing slick rock draws with ever-changing vistas. As the elevation increases, the views include Red Rock State Park, Cathedral Rock, Capitol Butte, Wilson Mountain, and Munds Mountain. Cross over a rise and descend toward the north face of House Mountain. At 1.5 miles, pass Turkey Creek Tank on the left, a cattle pond built up with a dirt mound. The road narrows to a footpath and crosses the Turkey Creek drainage. Walk up a side canyon, engulfed by the crescent-shaped wall in the curvature of House Mountain at 2.3 miles. Steeply ascend the mountain on the canyon's west wall. Zigzag up to the ridge and a junction in a saddle on the rim of the volcanic depression. From the unsigned junction are three options. The left fork heads east up the ridge, crossing a few plateaus to the 5,107-foot peak. Primitive, hand-made cairns mark the faint trail. The right fork heads west up the ridge to the 4,728-foot peak. The path is not marked, so follow the ridge along your own route. The main route, straight ahead, drops into the ancient crater, surrounded by forested hills with lava rock outcroppings.

CALDERA

▲ 5,127'

4,728'

5,107'

HOUSE MOUNTAIN

TURKEY CREEK

S W
E N

Turkey Creek

Turkey Creek
Tank

Oak Creek

RED ROCK
STATE PARK
HIKES 45–49

TRAIL

ROCK LOOP RD

TWIN
PILLARS

LOWER RED

P

95
BALDWIN
TRAIL

ALSO SEE MAPS ON
PAGES 105 • 170 • 209

TO
VILLAGE of
OAK CREEK

VERDE VALLEY SCHOOL RD

TURKEY CREEK TRAIL to
HOUSE MOUNTAIN

Hike 97
Jacks Canyon

Hiking distance: 7—13 miles round trip
Hiking time: 4—6.5 hours
Elevation gain: 1,000—2,000 feet
Maps: U.S.G.S. Munds Mountain
      Beartooth Publishing—Sedona, AZ

map
page 216

Summary of hike: Jacks Canyon is a 6.5-mile canyon in the Munds Mountain Wilderness, running from the Village of Oak Creek to Schnebly Hill. The forested canyon is tucked between Lee and Munds Mountains on the west and Horse Mesa on the east. Jacks Canyon Trail was built in the late 1800s to move livestock to the cooler summer pastures in the upper elevations. The trail is a strenuous hike that climbs from the mouth of the canyon to the Mogollon Rim, concluding at a 6,466-foot saddle between Munds Mountain and Schnebly Hill.

Driving directions: From the Sedona Y (Highways 89A and 179 junction), drive 7.2 miles south on Highway 179 (towards Phoenix), into the Village of Oak Creek, to Jacks Canyon Road. (The turnoff is 0.8 miles south of Bell Rock Boulevard.) Turn left and drive 2 miles to the posted turnoff on the right. Continue 100 yards to the large trailhead parking area.

Hiking directions: From the northeast corner of the parking area, pass through the trail gate. Walk northeast through an open forest of pines and cypress, with views of Lee Mountain and Courthouse Butte. Parallel Jacks Canyon Road between Horse Mesa and Lee Mountain, skirting around the Pines Valley subdivision. Climb past the last house, and drop to the canyon floor, leaving the development behind. The canyon walls slowly narrow and the trail curves north along the east side of Lee Mountain, parallel to the curvature of Horse Mountain. Continue up the old rocky road, reaching Jacks Canyon Tank (a stock pond) at 2.5 miles. Pass the east bank of the pond, and continue on the canyon floor. Enter the fenced Munds Mountain

Wilderness, and moderately ascend the canyon between sand-stone cliffs. This is a good turn-around spot for a 7- to 10-mile hike.

To continue hiking, ascend the canyon drainage, gaining 1,000 feet. The canyon changes from a forest of cypress, juni-per, and manzanita into Gambel oaks and ponderosa pines on the upper slope. Near the head of the canyon, steeply climb on fine white powder and tilted sandstone rock. Traverse the head of the canyon, with great views down the forested drainage and across the length of Munds Mountain. The trail ends on the 6,466-foot Munds Saddle at a junction. To the left is the Munds Mountain Trail (Hike 23). To the right is the Schnebly Hill Trail (Hike 22) and the Hot Loop Trail (Hike 98).

Hike 98
Hot Loop Trail

Hiking distance: 4.5—18 miles round trip
Hiking time: 2—9 hours
Elevation gain: 1,000—2,000 feet
Maps: U.S.G.S. Munds Mountain
      Beartooth Publishing—Sedona, AZ

map
page 216

Summary of hike: The Hot Loop Trail is a strenuous hike that climbs to the summit of Horse Mesa (also known as Wild Horse Mesa). The shadeless mesa rises between Jacks Canyon and Woods Canyon. Both canyons have an access route to the Hot Loop Trail. This hike begins from Jacks Canyon and climbs 1,000 feet to the top of Horse Mesa. The path crosses the broad, flat 5,200-foot plateau to the head of Jacks Canyon on the ridge between Munds Mountain and Schnebly Hill. Along the way are impressive vistas into the canyons and across to Lee Mountain and Munds Mountain. The trail continues several miles across the plateau to Munds Saddle.

Driving directions: From the Sedona Y (Highways 89A and 179 junction), drive 7.2 miles south on Highway 179 (towards Phoenix), into the Village of Oak Creek, to Jacks Canyon Road. (The turnoff is 0.8 miles south of Bell Rock Boulevard.) Turn left and drive 2 miles to the posted turnoff on the right. Continue 100 yards to the large trailhead parking area.

Hiking directions: Take the Hot Loop Trail from the far south end of the parking area, by the corral and loading chute. (The Jacks Canyon Trail begins from the northeast end of the parking area.) Head south towards the forested hill. Drop into a small gully by the metal trail sign at 200 yards. Curve around the west end of the forested foothill, leaving the mouth of Jacks Canyon. Pass a few homes and head up the hillside toward a distinct saddle on the ridge. Cross through the 4,500-foot saddle, and traverse the south-facing hillside, overlooking undeveloped Woods Canyon and the Village of Oak Creek. Cross slick rock beneath beautiful red rock formations, winding along the contours of the hillside. Drop into a side canyon, and cross a slab rock drainage to a T-junction with the Hot Loop Trail at 1.2 miles. The right fork connects with the Woods Canyon Trail (Hike 100), a second access route to Horse Mesa. Bear left and climb on scattered lava rock, passing the Hot Loop Tank on the right, to Horse Mesa. Enter the Munds Mountain Wilderness at just under 2 miles, and cross the plateau through a juniper and cypress forest. Side paths on the left lead to the south rim of Jacks Canyon, with views of the lower canyon, Munds Mountain, and Lee Mountain. This is a good turn-around spot for a 4.5 mile hike.

To hike farther, continue several miles north across the mesa between Jacks Canyon and Woods Canyon. The trail ends at the head of Jacks Canyon by a junction with the Schnebly Hill Trail, which heads sharply to the right (Hike 22). The Munds Mountain Trail (Hike 23) and Jacks Canyon Trail (Hike 97) head to the left. Choose your own turn-around spot anywhere along the expansive plateau.

To hike a loop and return through Jacks Canyon, take the left fork at the Schnebley Hill Trail junction. Head down the hill 80 yards to the 6,466-foot Munds Saddle and a junction. The Munds Mountain Trail climbs to the right; the Jacks Canyon Trail goes to the left. Continue hiking with the directions to Hike 99.

Hike 99
Hot Loop—Jacks Canyon Trail Loop

Hiking distance: 15.5 mile loop

Hiking time: 7.5 hours

Elevation gain: 2,000 feet

Maps: U.S.G.S. Munds Mountain
Beartooth Publishing—Sedona, AZ

map
next page

Summary of hike: The Hot Loop—Jacks Canyon Loop is a strenuous all-day hike. The route combines Hikes 97 and 98 for a scenic 15.5-mile loop between the Village of Oak Creek and Schnebly Hill. The trail climbs to the summit of Horse Mesa between Jacks Canyon and Woods Canyon, then crosses the massive plateau to the 6,466-foot ridge at the head of Jacks Canyon on the Mogollon Rim. The hike returns down the Jacks Canyon drainage between Munds Mountain, Lee Mountain, and Horse Mesa.

Driving directions: From the Sedona Y (Highways 89A and 179 junction), drive 7.2 miles south on Highway 179 (towards Phoenix), into the Village of Oak Creek, to Jacks Canyon Road. (The turnoff is 0.8 miles south of Bell Rock Boulevard.) Turn left and drive 2 miles to the posted turnoff on the right. Continue 100 yards to the large trailhead parking area.

Hiking directions: Follow the hiking directions for the Hot Loop Trail—Hike 98—to the 6,466-foot Munds Saddle at the head of Jacks Canyon. Take the left fork on the Jacks Canyon Trail, and steeply descend into the canyon on the fine white powder and tilted sandstone rock. The trail is tucked between Munds Mountain on the right and Horse Mesa on the left, with great views down the length of the forested canyon. Continue steadily downhill for miles. Exit the Munds Mountain Wilderness through a fenced opening, and pass the east edge of Jacks Canyon Tank (a stock pond). Descend on the rocky path, curving southeast along the curvature of Horse Mesa. Climb the hillside, skirting the southeast side of the Pines Valley subdivision.

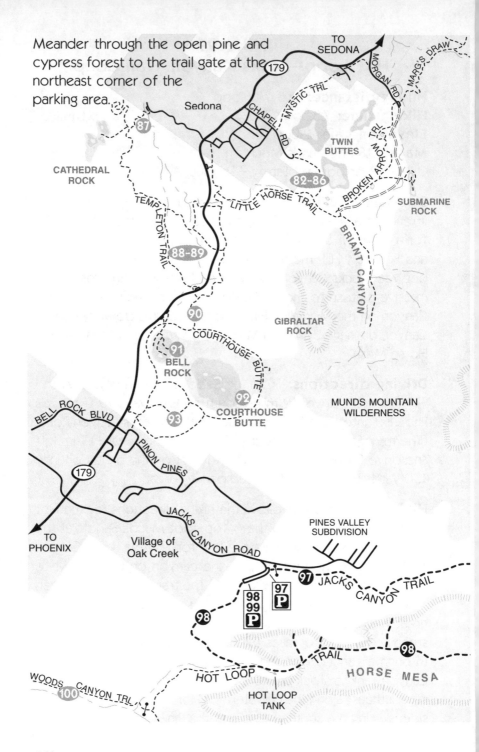

Meander through the open pine and cypress forest to the trail gate at the northeast corner of the parking area.

TO SEDONA

MARG'S DRAW

179

MORGAN RD

MYSTIC TRL

Sedona

CHAPEL RD

87

BROKEN ARROW TRL

TWIN BUTTES

CATHEDRAL ROCK

82-86

SUBMARINE ROCK

TEMPLETON TRAIL

LITTLE HORSE TRAIL

BRIANT CANYON

88-89

90

GIBRALTAR ROCK

COURTHOUSE BUTTE

91

BELL ROCK

MUNDS MOUNTAIN WILDERNESS

92

COURTHOUSE BUTTE

BELL ROCK BLVD

93

PINON PINES

179

JACKS CANYON ROAD

PINES VALLEY SUBDIVISION

TO PHOENIX

Village of Oak Creek

97

JACKS CANYON TRAIL

98
99
P

97
P

98

HOT LOOP

TRAIL

98

HORSE MESA

WOODS CANYON TRL

100

HOT LOOP TANK

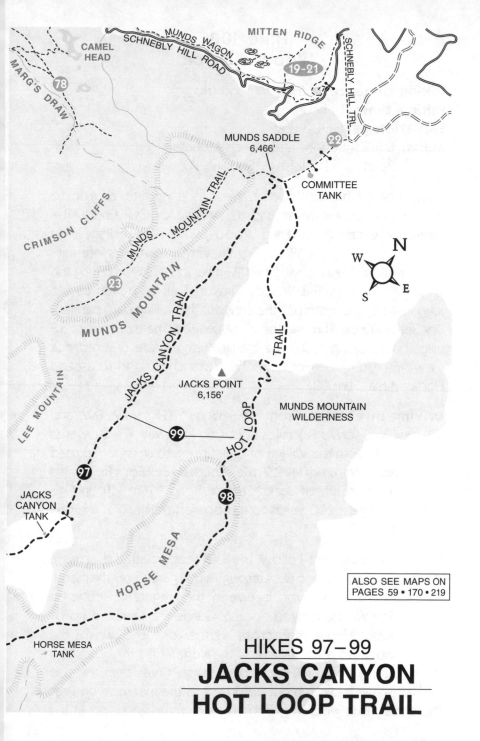

MITTEN RIDGE

MUNDS WAGON

SCHNEBLY HILL ROAD

CAMEL HEAD

SCHNEBLY HILL TRL.

MARG'S DRAW

(78)

19-21

MUNDS SADDLE
6,466'

(22)

COMMITTEE
TANK

CRIMSON CLIFFS

MUNDS MOUNTAIN TRAIL

MUNDS MOUNTAIN

(23)

JACKS CANYON TRAIL

HOT LOOP TRAIL

N
W   E
S

JACKS POINT
6,156'

MUNDS MOUNTAIN
WILDERNESS

LEE MOUNTAIN

(99)

HOT LOOP

(97)

(98)

JACKS
CANYON
TANK

HORSE MESA

ALSO SEE MAPS ON
PAGES 59 • 170 • 219

HORSE MESA
TANK

HIKES 97–99
JACKS CANYON
HOT LOOP TRAIL

Hike 100
Woods Canyon

Hiking distance: 6.6 miles round trip
Hiking time: 3.5 hours
Elevation gain: 300 feet
Maps: U.S.G.S. Sedona and Munds Mountain
      Beartooth Publishing—Sedona, AZ

Summary of hike: Woods Canyon is a remote canyon to the south of Horse Mesa and the Village of Oak Creek. The canyon was named for Fred Woods, who pastured sheep in the canyon during the 1880s. Dry Beaver Creek flows intermittently through the undeveloped 12-mile-long canyon during the winter and spring. The Woods Canyon Trail begins on an old jeep road at the mouth of the canyon. The rolling path parallels Dry Beaver Creek through the wide canyon. The trail ends at 3.3 miles on a sloping redrock expanse with picturesque redrock views. En route, the Hot Loop Trail branches north to ascend Horse Mesa (Hike 98).

Driving directions: From the Sedona Y (Highways 89A and 179 junction), drive 8.6 miles south on Highway 179 (towards Phoenix), through the Village of Oak Creek, to an unpaved road on the left. (The turnoff is 2.2 miles south of Bell Rock Boulevard and 1.4 miles south of Jacks Canyon Road.) Turn left and go through the gate 200 yards to the posted trailhead at the end of the road.

Hiking directions: Follow the old jeep road and cross a drainage. Curve east and pass through a trail gate. Enter the mouth of wide Woods Canyon between the vegetation-covered slopes. Follow the canyon floor towards the southern tip of Horse Mesa. At one mile, cross another drainage, where the road narrows to a footpath and the vegetation thickens. At 2 miles, enter a small slick rock side canyon. Cross over the slab rock drainage and climb out, returning to the main canyon. Pass through a cattle gate, and climb 40 yards to a signed fork at the foot of Horse Mesa. The Hot Loop Trail veers left and climbs to the plateau atop Horse Mesa (Hike 98). Continue straight on the right fork, staying in Woods Canyon. Follow the north canyon wall along red rock cliffs through a forest of sycamores, cottonwoods, oaks, and cypress. Slowly descend to the creek, which can carry a large volume of water in the spring. At 3 miles are views up Rattlesnake Canyon to the east. Emerge on a red, slick rock shelf at 3.3 miles. During the winter and spring, numerous pools line the area. Beyond this scenic spot, the trail fades and scrambles over rocks. Return by retracing your steps.

HORSE MESA TANK

HORSE MESA

MUNDS MOUNTAIN WILDERNESS

JACKS CANYON TRAIL

97

98

HOT LOOP TANK

98

JACKS CANYON ROAD

Village of Oak Creek

HOT LOOP TRAIL

RATTLESNAKE CANYON

TO SEDONA

TRAIL

WOODS CANYON

Dry Beaver Creek

N
E
W
S

TO PHOENIX

179

P

ALSO SEE MAPS ON PAGES 170 • 216

WOODS CANYON

DAY HIKE BOOKS

These books may be purchased at your local bookstore or outdoor shop. Or, order them directly from the distributor:

National Book Network

800-462-6420

DAY HIKES ON THE
**California
Central
Coast**
120 COASTAL HIKES FROM
SANTA CRUZ TO SANTA BARBARA
Robert Stone

DAY HIKES ON THE
**California
Southern
Coast**
100 GREAT HIKES
Robert Stone

DAY HIKES IN THE
**Santa Monica
Mountains**
FROM LOS ANGELES TO POINT MUGU
INCLUDING THE ENTIRE BACKBONE TRAIL
Robert Stone

DAY HIKES AROUND
**Sonoma
County**
125 GREAT HIKES
Robert Stone

DAY HIKES AROUND
**Napa
Valley**
88 GREAT HIKES
Robert Stone

DAY HIKES AROUND
**Monterey
& Carmel**
125 GREAT HIKES
Robert Stone

DAY HIKES AROUND
Big Sur
99 GREAT HIKES
Robert Stone
2nd EDITION

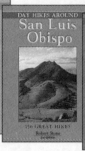
DAY HIKES AROUND
**San Luis
Obispo**
156 GREAT HIKES
Robert Stone
2nd EDITION

DAY HIKES AROUND
**Santa
Barbara**
116 GREAT HIKES
Robert Stone
4th EDITION

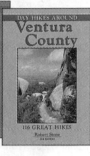
DAY HIKES AROUND
**Ventura
County**
116 GREAT HIKES
Robert Stone
2nd EDITION

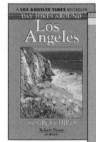
A LOS ANGELES TIMES BESTSELLER
DAY HIKES AROUND
**Los
Angeles**
160 GREAT HIKES
Robert Stone
4th EDITION

DAY HIKES AROUND
**Orange
County**
112 GREAT HIKES
Robert Stone
3rd EDITION

DAY HIKES IN
Yosemite
NATIONAL PARK
80 GREAT HIKES
Robert Stone
3rd EDITION

DAY HIKES IN
**Sequoia
&
Kings Canyon**
NATIONAL PARKS
Robert Stone

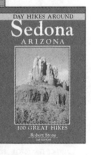
DAY HIKES AROUND
Sedona
ARIZONA
100 GREAT HIKES
Robert Stone
2nd EDITION

DAY HIKES IN
Yellowstone
NATIONAL PARK
82 GREAT HIKES
Robert Stone
4th EDITION

DAY HIKES IN
**Grand
Teton**
NATIONAL PARK
89 GREAT HIKES
Robert Stone
4th EDITION

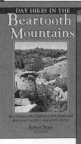
DAY HIKES IN THE
**Beartooth
Mountains**
RED LODGE MT. TO YELLOWSTONE
BEARTOOTH VALLEY AND PARADISE VALLEY
Robert Stone
2nd EDITION

DAY HIKES AROUND
Bozeman
MONTANA
INCLUDING THE GALLATIN
CANYON AND PARADISE VALLEY
Robert Stone

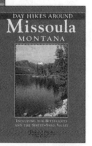
DAY HIKES AROUND
Missoula
MONTANA
INCLUDING THE BITTERROOTS
AND THE SEELEY-SWAN VALLEY
Robert Stone

ADRIENNE METTER

About the Author

Since 1991, Robert Stone has been writer, photographer, and publisher of Day Hike Books. He is a Los Angeles Times Best Selling Author and an award-winning journalist of Rocky Mountain Outdoor Writers and Photographers, the Outdoor Writers Association of California, the Northwest Outdoor Writers Association, the Outdoor Writers Association of America, and the Bay Area Travel Writers. Robert has hiked every trail in the Day Hike Book series. With 20 hiking guides in the series, many in their fourth and fifth editions, he has hiked thousands of miles of trails throughout the western United States. When Robert is not hiking, he researches, writes, and maps the hikes before returning to the trails. He spends summers in the Rocky Mountains of Montana and winters on the California Central Coast.